MUSINGS ON GLOBAL POLITICS

NAVEED QAZI

ISBN 13: 978-1984209979
ISBN-10: 1984209973

Formatting, proofreading and editing done by the author.

Typeset in Adobe Caslon Pro

Cover design also by Naveed Qazi.

www.naveedqazi.com

Paperback and digital editions available from Kindle Direct Publishing, an Amazon unit.

UK | US | Australia | Italy | Spain | India | Netherlands
Japan | Brazil | Canada | Germany | Mexico | UAE
Singapore | Turkey | Poland | China | Saudi Arabia

kindle
direct
publishing

A collection of selected newspaper columns and other
political essays

CONTENTS

ABBREVIATIONS

ANC African National Congress
AfD *Alternative für Deutschland (German)*
ASEAN Association of Southeast Asian Nations
AMISOM African Union Mission to Somalia
AKP *Adalet ve Kalkinma Partisi (Turkish)*
BDS Boycott, Divestment and Sanctions
BJP *Bharatiya Janata Party (Hindi)*
BRICS Brazil Russia India China South Africa
BBC British Broadcasting Corporation
COFADEH Committee of Relatives of the Detained-Disappeared in Honduras
CDU Christian Democratic Union
CSU Christian Socialist Union
CPEC China Pakistan Economic Corridor
CPI Communist Party of India
CRIF *Conseil Représentatif des Institutions juives de France (French)*
CNRP Cambodia National Rescue Party
CIA Central Intelligence Agency
CSR Corporate Social Responsibility
CUP *Candidatura d'Unitat Popular (Spanish)*
DUP Democratic Unionist Party
DA Democratic Alliance
DDPD Doha Document for Peace in Darfur
DFID Department for International Development
EU European Union
EEU Euro Asian Economic Union
ECOWAS Economic Community of West African States
ENI European Neighbourhood Instrument
FARC *Fuerzas Armadas Revolucionarias de Colombia (Spanish)*
FEDECAMARAS *Federación de Cámaras y Asociaciones*

de Comercio y Producción de Venezuela (Spanish)
FIFA *Fédération Internationale de Football Association (French)*
FDI Foreign Direct Investment
FSA Free Syrian Army
GNA Government of National Accord
GATT General Agreements on Tariffs and Trade
GDP Gross Domestic Product
HIA *Hezb-e-Islami Afghanistan (Arabic)*
HoR House of Representatives
ISIS Islamic State of Iraq & Syria
ICCPR International Covenant on Civil and Political Rights
ICESCR International Covenant on Economic, Social and Cultural Rights
IMF International Monetary Fund
IRGC Iran Revolutionary Guard Corps
IB Intelligence Bureau
ICIJ International Consortium of Investigative Journalists
JBS Jose Batista Sobrinho
JTF Joint Task Force
KDF Kenyan Defence Forces
KRG Kurdistan Regional Government
LPA Libyan Peace Agreement
MAP Membership Action Plan
MADJ *Movimiento Amplio por la Dignidad y la Justicia (Spanish)*
MP Member Parliament
MoU Memorandum of Understanding
NATO North Atlantic Treaty Organisation
NMDC National Mineral Development Corporation
NGO Non-Governmental Organisation
NLD National League for Democracy
NLJP National Liberation and Justice Party
PMDB *Partido do Movimento Democrático Brasileiro (Portuguese)*

PiS *Prawo i Sprawiedliwosc (Polish)*
PO *Platforma Obywatelska (Polish)*
PLO Palestinian Liberation Organisation
PJAK *Partiya Jiyana Azad a Kurdistanê (Kurdish)*
RAW Research and Analysis Wing
RIL Reliance Industries Limited
SAARC South Asian Association for Regional Cooperation
SLAPP Strategic Litigation Against Public Participation
SNSC Supreme National Security Council
SSBN Submarine Ballistic Nuclear Powered
SLM Sudan Liberation Movement
THAAD Terminal High Altitude Area Defence
TPP Trans Pacific Partnership Agreement
TSE *Tribunal Supremo Electoral (Spanish)*
UAE United Arab Emirates
USD United States Dollar
US United States
UK United Kingdom
UNFCCC United Nations Framework Convention on Climate Change
UNCLOS United Nations Convention on the Law of the Sea
UGTT *Union Générale Tunisienne du Travail (French)*
UNAMID African Union-United Nations Hybrid Operation in Darfur
UPA United Progressive Alliance
WTO World Trade Organisation
WDM World Development Movement
YPG *Yekineyen Parastina Gel (Kurdish)*
ZANU PF Zimbabwe African National Union Patriotic Front

1

THE WORLD IS RUNNING OUT OF COCOA

THE INTERNATIONAL DEMAND has risen tremendously in recent years.

As there is low supply and high demand, it had resulted in a price rise, and the scenario, forced many cocoa beans grinding units to close their operations.

The price of cocoa has increased, due to the Ebola crisis and weather conditions, such as El Nino, when ocean temperatures rise, in the eastern Pacific. However, since 2017, there seems to be a slump in cocoa prices.

Countries, such as the Ivory Coast, have been heavily dependent on cocoa production. It produces the world's 40 per cent of cocoa. Around seven million people are associated with the industry.

Big companies such as Mars, The Hershey Company, and Nestle, mostly use Ivorian cocoa to produce their chocolate, and have been expanding into the region.

The farmers, in Ivory Coast, have destroyed, around thirty-four thousand hectares of land, because they are planning to make parks and reserves. Young farmers are no longer interested, in planting cocoa, while as old farmers are reaching their life expectancy. Add to that, most of the world's cocoa farmers, live in extreme poverty.

To save forests, the government is also trying to expel many farmers. They are starting the initiative from Mont Peko, an area that has an illegal population, of around twenty-eight thousand people. Child labour has been another problem, on western African cocoa farms.

Analysts have often attributed a rise in illegal cocoa farming, in Ivory Coast, which is now getting curbed.

According to local cocoa farmers, hundreds of police, and paramilitaries, have also burned the crops, on a massive scale. All these factors might further decrease the production of cocoa beans.
Ivorian Coast introduced a forward sales system, in 2012. Unlike big companies, this system created a problem for smaller companies, because they could not hedge their purchases. As local companies speculated a lot, some big companies made money, while others could not. It led to a grim situation lately, as the Ivorian Cocoa Exporters Association revealed that they had a chance to default, on around 80,000 tonnes of export contracts.

In March 2011, prices were at a 32-year high, before falling forty-two per cent, by the end of the year. The cocoa prices recovered, in 2014, amidst many industry concerns, about a cocoa bean shortage. Such fluctuation, in prices, means cocoa farmers cannot predict how much they will get for their beans. They cannot even plan for their future nicely. This makes the cocoa business not lucrative.

Due to the political upheavals, production has also been affected due to ten years of civil unrest, in the Ivory Coast. In terms of production, the country's closest rival is Ghana, followed by Indonesia, Ecuador, and Cameroon.

One of the main reasons, for the declining cocoa

production, has been the ageing trees. There also seems to be less supply of fertilisers available to farmers. The tree tends to grow in shade and has specific climatic and rainfall requirements.

Whenever there has been a bad season, fungal diseases happen, which include the 'black pod disease,' and 'swollen shoot disease,' and the disease reduces the plant productivity, and the diseases kill the tree, in two years. It may eventually impact the whole regional market, and so will the pollution, due to the illegal mining of gold.

As miners look for gold, in streams and other water bodies, they use mercury, cyanide, and other complex chemicals, to extract gold from places. Heavy metals, released during the process, seep into the soil, of nearby cocoa farms, reducing their productivity, and making the crop hazardous.

The cocoa industry, in Africa is troubled by other factors, that include limited access to credit, and the shift towards rubber production, a decision taken by many African farmers.

In Ghana, around $3 billion is earned on cocoa production. The Sehwi area in Ghana, which is the heart of cocoa production, has poor access to roads.

However, many press reports have been on the radar that alleges the government not paying enough bonuses, to the farmers. The Bank of Ghana data shows that between February 2016 and 2017, Ghana's revenue from cocoa exports dropped, by 10 per cent.

According to statistics, the world's biggest cocoa port lies on the coast of San Pedro, on Ivory Coast. There have been cases where buyers have not paid the farmers. Some

80 per cent of buyers have backed out, of their contracts, due to the increased price of cocoa, set by the government.

With the result, initiatives like Fairtrade aim to make cocoa farming a more sustainable way, to earn a living, so that farmers can better support themselves, and their families.

The aim is to help farmers, in workshops, by making them learn, how to negotiate contracts with traders. Fairtrade's Minimum Price for cocoa is set at $2,000 per ton, and for each ton, the farmer organisation receives an extra $200 Fairtrade Premium.

The farmer, to improve the efficiency, of the organisation's farms, or to increase the yields, and quality of their cocoa, in community projects, can invest in this incentive.

Quite lately, the Dominican Republic, which is known for producing high-grade, organic-flavoured cocoa, has assured of strengthening its sector, for around 40,000 farmers.

Despite the love of North Americans, and Europeans, for chocolate, the demand for chocolate has skyrocketed, in Asia too, as the Chinese, are rediscovering their cultural tastes.

28 January, 2018

2

STRATEGIC LITIGATIONS AGAINST PUBLIC PARTICIPATION

To CENSURE ACTIVISTS AND OPPONENTS, Indian corporates, for a while, have been using legal protection, against journalists and campaigners.

Strategic Litigation Against Public Participation (SLAPP) has become an instrument, where the powerful, dictate terms to the lesser privileged, for their freedom of speech. Most commonly, they arise as defamation suits.

Almost three years back, the RIL lawyers filed a complaint about token damage, of up to '100 crore,' in ten days, against the authors of *Gas Wars: Crony Capitalism and the Ambanis* (2014). The antagonists in this book, the Ambanis, had called the charges, laid down against them, as 'derogatory.'

The kind of narrative, published in *Gas Wars* (2014), had been quite different, from what the common masses heard about Reliance Industries. The adversarial views, on RIL, led to the company's *'Streisand Effect.'*

In public, RIL had been an entity, which had seemingly changed the corporate image of India globally, with its innovative approaches, such as shared ownership, amidst the middle class, to keep RIL dividends rising.

Gas Wars (2014) alleged that Ambanis had put pressure on the Congress-led government, to change ministerial portfolios to suit RIL's needs.

There have been different controversies, surrounding the pricing and utilisation, of the Krishna Godavari gas fields, too.

The three authors of *Gas Wars* (2014) namely, Subir Ghosh, Paranjoy Guha Thakurta, and Jyotirmoy Chaudhuri, claim that the notices put against them did not point out a 'single factual error,' of what had been published by them.

Sue the Messenger (2016) restates that the claims, made in the book *Gas Wars* (2014), were about the division of the two brothers, in a long battle, over the supply of natural gas, from the Krishna-Godaveri basin.

Hamish McDonald, an Australian journalist, described the journalists, close to Ambanis as a 'dirty dozen,' and 'moles in the press,' who were dedicated to getting favourable news, about the corporate. In short, they seemed to be their marketers.

The tussle between Reliance Industries and journalists goes back long. When *The Polyester Prince* (1998) was published by Hamish McDonald, the lawyers of Reliance, in Australia (Ashurst Australia) had sent defamation notices, to their publisher, Allen and Unwin, warning them of stern action, in case of defamation.

The legal threat had ironically come before the book was published.

Around December 2013, another high-profile legal battle emerged, after the filing of a 200 crore-defamation suit, by Sahara India Parivar, in Calcutta High Court, where they alleged 'defamatory content,' from a Mint journalist.

Scroll journalist, Supriya Sharma recently put forward a breaking news story, where Essar Group had signed an MoU with the Chhattisgarh state government, to open a steel plant, in Bastar.

The government had allowed a mining lease, of iron ore, at discounted prices from National Mineral Development Corporation (NMDC). The iron ore was mixed with slurry, and water, and passed through a 257-kilometre pipeline, through Vishakapatnam, Andra Pradesh. The logistic costs had significantly come down, but these pipelines passed through Maoist areas.

In July 2010, a cable from the US consulate in Mumbai, released by Wikileaks, revealed that Essar Group had been bribing Maoists, in significant amounts, to not interfere, in their operations. When one group of Maoists retaliated, Essar Group allegedly formed a counter-Maoist group, to defend their interests.

SLAPPs have reflected the desperation of corporates, to make things run smoothly, in their favour.

Essar denied these charges all along, but when the General Manager of Essar Steel, DVCS Varma was arrested under the Indian Penal Code, under Section 121 and Section 124 (A), along with BK Lala, (a building contractor tasked with repairing a pipeline blown up by Maoists in 2009) with ₹15 lakhs, new controversies had emerged. It is because Essar called itself a law-abiding corporate. Nevertheless, a case had been filed against Essar, for supporting the Maoists.

The Essar Group, also filed a defamation suit, against Green Peace worth 500 crores, on 28th January 2014. They filed it for a perched banner named 'We Kill Forests,' near Essar headquarters, in Mumbai. A recent report filed by IB (Intelligence Bureau) stated that Greenpeace activists worked against the interests of India, and violated the Foreign Contribution Regulation Act (2010). Essar also used this IB report against Greenpeace activists.

When the story, 'India Cut Rose Sector Pushes Past Barriers' was published on 18th July 2014, reflecting Karuturi Global's business practices, a legal notice was sent to its author, a Bengaluru-based freelancer, Keya Acharya, by a legal firm, called Pastay Law. The notice claimed that the author had put Karuturi, and his family members, in an embarrassing situation.

They asked Acharaya for an unconditional apology, including two 50 crore suits, for 'damage for loss of reputation,' and 'mental agony.'

In November 2014, in Addis-Ababa, an IPS report alleged, how Karuturi Global, the world's largest producer of cut roses, minted money, by exporting sugarcane, through Ethiopian child labour. Intelligence Bureau (IB) alleged the corporate of insider trading, in December 2010.

India has been inured by this practice, for quite some time. There have been books written, extensive reportages done, and long form articles, drafted in magazines, but the debate, on this issue, somehow, has not taken off, possibly because of fear.

23 January, 2018

3

TUNISIAN DEMOCRACY IN DANGER

T HOUSANDS OF TUNISIANS HAVE gathered on the streets of Tunis in January, 2018, to mark the anniversary of the ousting of former President Ben Ali, who went into exile to Saudi Arabia in January 2011.

This had been the country, where the 2011 Arab Spring had started, against a tyrannical rule. Protests were churning out in Tunisia, in 2016, too, on unemployment, in the Kasserine region. Then in 2017, there was the Kamour movement, in the south, which ended after the government accepted demands.

Right now, the country is running a fragile government. They have promised that the common people will reap the fruits of prosperity, mainly from foreign investments, but Tunisians do not believe their leaders.

Since 1956, Tunisia has followed an economic model that has focused entirely on cheap exports, to Europe, and on budget mass tourism, for Europeans.

The prime minister, president, and the senate hold equal power. At the same time, social activists are active, in civil society organisations, and labour unions. There has been a change in thinking for institutionalising policy and reforms, but it is not worthwhile, as there are security threats, coming from jihadists, illegal migration, and from smuggling.

Press reports have shown stories, where even 50-year-olds, have joined the protests, for freedom and dignity.

Backers, of an Islamist Revolution party, called *Ennahda,* which took power several years, after the revolution, have called for its return to power.

For a couple of days, they have been dominating several concert scenes, where episodes of loud music have been reported. Vendors have been busy selling Tunisian flags, to the public.

A new law increasing prices of daily commodities, including an increase in value-added tax, has fuelled the unrest.

Economists believe, that suspending the finance law, can likely slow down the economy, even more.

Many children were also among those waving flags, singing and dancing, and their parents have been unusually unconcerned about the prolonged violence in the past. The consequences may seem harsh and alarming, but Tunisians are continuing to fight for their ideals.

There is perceived anger in Tunisia, because of low employment prospects, dwindling economy and corruption.

Many factory workers have flared up the sentiments, of trade unions, who are also joining the protests. The powerful UGTT labour union has demanded a call for pay increases and a higher minimum wage. It seems that Tunisia, is in a boiling pot, again.

In 2015, terror attacks ruined tourism, in Tunisia, where

an ISIS-trained gunman had been trained, for the plot, in Libya.

The tourism industry makes up only 8 per cent of the GDP, in the country, but more than 440,000 British tourists travelled annually, to Tunisian beaches, and archaeological sites, before the Sousse attack, but in its aftermath, there has been a 90% fall.

This makes the situation, in the country, even direr.

Prime Minister, Youssef Chahed decided to reimburse around 100 million dinars (about USD 40 million), to help nearly 200,000 needy Tunisian families, plus free health care, for the jobless.

An aid fund for poor families, to acquire housing, also was created, but the Popular Front, a leftist coalition, denounced this move, stating that unless and until the buying power of people does not improve, no such welfare measure could become successful.

Journalists from Tunisia have reported about dozens of police cars, that have been damaged, two police stations have also been burned, and eight others have been ransacked.

Arrests have been put at nearly 780, including 16 religious' extremists, for vandalism and looting.

The Tunisian Revolution in 2011 was sparked by the death of a fruit and vegetable seller, in the central town of Sidi Bouzid, who set himself afire, in apparent anger and despairs, over mistreatment by police, who upset his cart. These wounds of social mistreatment, are still fresh, among the Tunisians.

Since then, a four-way peace making group, known as the Tunisian National Dialogue Quartet, had been tasked to initiate dialogue, in an attempt, to build a pluralistic democracy, in Tunisia.

The entity was later awarded the 2015 Nobel Peace Prize, 'for its decisive contribution, to building a pluralistic democracy, in Tunisia.'

But, it seems, some hard work needs to be done, if the stakeholders want to achieve some practical means, to initiate the peace process. It is because the political protests have started again. On the grassroots level, the Tunisians seem to be unhappy.

In the past, the dictatorship that was established in the 1950s, transformed Tunisia into a police state later. It banned politics, and pushed Tunisians away from their public affairs.

A recent poll published, by the International Republican Institute, has found that an overwhelming majority of Tunisians consider the economic situation 'very bad.'

Current austerity measures, and tax increases, drafted by the government, have been demanded by the IMF, which is Tunisia's biggest lender.

It has granted the country €2.4 billion ($2.93 billion) in loans, up to 2020. The government aims to reduce its budget, to less than 6 per cent.

It might reflect Tunisia's lending capabilities, as well. In Tunisia, bank loans are often available, only to public servants, or others, with stable salaries.

Other ordinary individuals are sometimes required to give highly demanding guarantees.

These important concerns, rising, might bring the old ways of dictatorship, seen before the 2011 Jasmine Revolution, back into their political scene.

15 January, 2018

4

PALESTINE THROUGH THE EYES OF DISSENTERS

THE SLAPPING OF AN ISRAELI SOLDIER, by a sixteen-year-old activist, Ahed Tamimi, in December 2017, has become a new symbol of Palestinian resistance.

While her cousin, Nour Tamimi had been released, on bail, for 5000 *shekels* (1400 USD), Ahed has been charged, with twelve counts, and if found guilty, could be convicted, for a longer jail presence.

Her mother, who filmed the video, has also been charged. In 2015, Ahed bit a hand of an Israeli soldier, to try to stop the arrest of her brother.

This young activist comes from a prominent Tamimi family, residing in the village of Nabi Saleh, who are renowned for their political activism.

Ahed's father wants her to become the poster child, of the most significant Palestinian peaceful resistance movement, namely Boycott, Divestment and Sanctions (BDS).

To many, Ahed is seen as the West Bank's Joan of Arc. Interestingly, the media has not given her as much worldwide attention, as Pakistani activist Malala Yousufzai.

According to Middle East-based journalist, Caroline Glick, the Tamimi family has been leading the global war against Israel, in recent times.

The journalist claims that Tamimi's have connections with the Israeli and American Left, the EU, Jordan, Hamas, and PLO.

The family also have claimed to enjoy the support, from all dissenting quarters of the globe. But the family has also been involved in direct murders, and not only political activism.

Ahed's aunt, Ahlam Tamimi, plotted the massacre, at a Sbarro pizzeria, in Jerusalem. She chose this landmark place because it was popular among families, with young children.

She brought a suicide bomber, to the restaurant, where he blew himself up, killing fifteen people, among them seven children, and wounding one hundred thirty people.

Ahlam and Nizar, Ahed's extended family members, were released in 2011, as part of Israel's '1,000-terrorists-for-one-hostage-soldier Gilad Schalit deal.' Ahed had been a part of their marriage ceremony, and this wedding had been celebrated, on the Jordanian media.

When Ahed Tamimi addressed three-year-old graders, in New York, she sanctioned extremism against the Israeli state.

The Turkish state also recently awarded the Tamimi family recognition, in Ankara. Ahed has been awarded '*Hanzala Award for Courage*' by Turkey.

Making war seems so common with the Palestinians. It reflects their deepest sense of anger against the Israeli state. Palestinian teenagers typically face about six to nine months in prison for charges of stone-throwing.

Prisoners' rights group, Addameer, has reported that stone-throwing is the most common charge sanctioned against Palestinian children. In the occupied West Bank, Palestinians are governed by Israeli military law, and stone-throwing in this territory is punishable by up to 20 years in prison.

The Addameer group believes that Israel routinely targets 'the youngest and most vulnerable' members of politically active Palestinian families to 'exert pressure on their family and the entire community to put an end to all social mobilisation.'

Prof. Gerald Steinberg of the NGO monitor believes that the agenda 'Cross-border Cooperation within the European Neighbourhood Instrument (ENI): 'Mediterranean Sea Basin Program 2014-2020,' has been serving as an instrument for the EU, to continue to transfer millions of euros each year to anti-Israel groups, to carry out its war of subversion against Israel, and its democratic system.

Since 1995, Steinberg noted: 'the EU has used previous versions of this agreement to transfer tens of millions of euros to extremism supporting groups, and groups actively involved in Israeli politics, and inciting Israel's Arab community to join the war against the Jewish state.'

Palestine has been often called, as the mother of all conflicts, because of its religious significance.

The Israeli state is axing its toe, repeatedly, by provoking common Palestinians, who are also natives of this worn torn territory. Thousands have been killed, orphaned, injured, and live a life of psychological despair, in the brutalities of war. Air raids, food shortages, and ceasefire violations, still ravage common life.

As most of the common Palestinians live in exile, Israel cannot afford to 'theocratise' its Jewish state policy further, based on its religious scriptures. It will further radicalise the Palestinians. The Israeli state needs to realise that the place has a religious significance, for other faiths, too.

In 2017 alone, Israel seized around 2,500 acres of Palestinian land. Israelis arrested more than 6000 Palestinians, in the same year. Around 900 cases of violence have been reported, in 2017, by the Israeli forces, in East Jerusalem's *Al-Aqsa* Mosque.

The current Israeli policy is a policy against pluralism and is discriminating against other communities. The central committee of Netanyahu's *Likud* Party has recently backed a resolution, where they intend to reinstate Israeli military occupation, to all areas of West Bank, and initiate permanent settlement, through construction.

It is believed that Israel wants to bring the number of settlers, in the West Bank, to a million, in a short period, while half a million residents are currently living, in Jewish settlements, on Palestinian soil, and 220,000 in the settlements, in East Jerusalem.

Ironic it may seem, but the hopes of a two-state solution, are also dwindling. The US state administration still fully supports the Israeli state policy and the important question remains: where is the scope of a result-oriented political dialogue?

2 February, 2018

5

DARFUR MEDIATION: POLITICS OF ILLUSION

IN DARFUR, WESTERN SUDAN, the hostilities have been decreasing, since 2009, but there is no peace in sight.

The number of rebel factions, and armed movements, has made it a complex situation, leading to stark ethnic, and religious divisions. For years, this rebel movement, in Darfur, has been bred, on local support.

On 29 March 2017, the African Union-United Nations Hybrid Operation (UNAMID), discussed the Darfur meditation.

At this meeting, they noted improvement, in the situation, and called for a review, of the 'deployment of the mission, in the context of the improved environment, in Darfur.'

There has been no comprehensive peace agreement, in Darfur, until now. The Darfur conflict, started in 2003, when two rebel movements took up arms, to protest the economic and political marginalisation in Sudan.

Violence, in the Darfur region, of Sudan's far west, continues unabated. Some 450,000 persons have been displaced, in 2014, and another 100,000, in January 2015. The new Rapid Support Forces (RSF) has worsened violence and displacements.

Over time, two peace agreements have been drafted, namely the Darfur Peace Agreement, of 2006, and the Doha Document of Peace, in Darfur (DDPD), in 2011. However, neither of them has been signed by all the rebel groups.

At this point, the government in Sudan, still views the DDPD, as the framework for any resolution. The rebel groups reject this document because they view it as being 'too favourable,' to the government.

Since 2015, there have been instances of ceasefires announced for over six months, by the Sudan Liberation Movement (SLM) and Sudan People's Liberation Movement. In December 2017, National Liberation and Justice Party (NLJP), led by Tijani al-Sissi, called on the African mediation, to resume Darfur peace talks.

It seems that there is a lack of a coherent legal framework, that can guide this place, to any peaceful settlement. In June 2016, the Sudanese government also declared a four-month ceasefire, extended for two months, in October, another in December, and recently for six months, in January 2017.

From the point of view, of the government, these political actions were necessary, to convince the outgoing Obama administration, to lift the 20-year-long US sanctions against Sudan. But it remains unclear how this fourteen-year conflict will reach an end through current talks, mediated by the African Union and UN.

The peacekeeping mission, in Darfur, is known to be one of the costliest, with a budget of more than $1billion.
In Darfur, conflicts at the local level persist, between Arab and non-Arab militias. These groups fight for gold, in

places, such as the Jebel Mara. Many swathes of land have become vacant, and around two million people, have been displaced.

Darfur's ethnic tribes, the Fur and Zaghawa, have complained of getting fewer political rights, than the dominant Arab tribes, who live side by side.

Most problems, in Darfur, have been made worse, by the refugee crisis, and desertification, from climate change. One can find dead animals, in the middle of deserted villages, during the day.

Some clashes can also grow out of personal disagreements that could regularly be addressed, by legal mechanisms, like courts—which may be ineffective, or non-existent, in remote areas. Police, in this situation, do nothing.

On the contrary, people benefit from each other, unjustly, through a deep sense of tribalism.

The *hakkamat*, Sudan's traditional female singers, and poets are war agitators, who instigate their fellow tribesmen, to go to battle. This practice of provocation continues to date, despite ongoing appeals, from activists, to change the custom.

There was a referendum, held in April 2016, on the Darfur area's administrative status. Originally a federal state, Darfur had been divided, into three states, in 1994, and then into five states.

During the referendum, 97% of voters chose the 'states option' over the 'regional option'. This meant that Darfur would remain divided into five states.

The referendum was strongly criticised, by many stakeholders, and political observers, because of the security context, which did not allow internally displaced persons, and refugees, to participate, in the referendum. The organisation, of this poll, also raised questions, about the government's commitment, to address the grievances, that led to the Darfur conflict.

Mediation efforts, by the Sudanese government, and other parties, have failed to reverse the collective resignation, of Darfuri students, from the Bakht al-Rida University, in the White Nile state, in the past.

In a resolution, adopted, in 2000, the United Nations Security Council declared that women and children are most affected, by armed conflict, in Darfur.

They stressed the importance of women's participation, in peace-building and reconciliation.

But, in a survey conducted a decade later, the UN concluded there has been 'little success,' and that women made up less than 10 per cent, of those involved, in formal peace negotiations.

That is why the Crises Group, in 2014, gave several recommendations, including unfettered humanitarian access, developing concerns, for all communities, progressive demilitarisation, and leaving mediation, to respected neutral Sudanese.

This whole scenario, indicated, that several processes, need to be revived, modified, and reinitiated, especially in the UN Security Council, on Darfur.

28 December, 2017

6

A WAY FORWARD WITH NEPAL ELECTIONS

THE 2017 ELECTION, THE COUNTRY'S FIRST since 1999, has paved a new way, for the establishment of democracy, in Nepal.

It is an ambitious nation, where politicians, and political parties, subscribe, largely, to Marxist ideas. This election has made the transition of the country, from a unitary system to a federal state.

The leaders, of Marxist alliance, namely KP Oli, and Prachanda, were once bitter enemies, but now, the alliance will form the government, in six out of seven states.

There had been violence, just a few days, before the election, when Maoist militants, opened fire on politicians, blew up vehicles, planted landmines, and targeted civilians, in dozens of attacks, injuring at least 17 people.

The ruling alliance, Nepali Congress, was shocked to see both rivals joining hands, in the aftermath, of the election. Although, power bargaining for key posts, including the speakers, and several key minister posts, will remain a cause of disagreement, in the coming time.

The country has already called China, for investments, to build trans-Himalayan railways. The alliance might also bring a hydro-electrical project, modelled on the Three

Gorges Dam, funded by the Chinese, back into operation, in the coming time.

During the 1990s, when underground Leftist parties, launched a democracy movement, it got support from major Indian political parties, only opposed by the BJP.

Through this democratic transition, common Nepalis demand good governance, an end to corruption, a pace in development projects, and welfare for the victims of 'Gorkha Earthquake,' which killed over 9,000 people, and injured over 22,000 people.

Nepal still struggles with basic infrastructures, such as schools and hospitals. Its courts, police, and civil administration, still lag far behind, in operating, at an efficient level. There are still prevailing deep-seated political rivalries, ethnic, and religious divides, and a lack of justice, for victims, of war crimes.

However, the good news, coming from the recently concluded election, has been the reservation of women seats (around thirty-three per cent), which reflects Nepal's concern about gender equality, in south Asia.

When King Birendra, led the monarchy, in 1985, the country had annulled a Chinese tender, for the construction of the 204-kilometer Kohalpur-Banbasa road, just because the King wanted to align with India, if Chinese, and Indian interests, clashed. Now, the political situation, in the country, has changed.

In the past, Nepal faced a ten-year-old civil war (1996-2006), when leftist rebels, tried to overthrow the monarchy, until the enactment of the Comprehensive Peace Accord, signed, in 2006. During that time, about 19,000 people were killed, including the armed forces. 150,000 civilians were internally displaced.

During the civil war, the Marxist militia, regarded the monarchy, as a 'feudal force.'

The monarchy, during the civil war, imprisoned journalists, closed newspapers, and rejected the demands of militia, wanting to become part of the legislative assembly.

During that period, many Nepalis migrated to Gulf countries, for jobs, to make a living, and for the fear of mass killings.

The recently concluded election may be bad news for India, which has for years, tried to exert its political influence, in the country. In 2017, Nepal signed and endorsed Beijing's *'One Belt, One Road plan'* – a project that connects the Eurasian landmass with China, where the country is giving loans, at concessional rates. The agreement would further cement Nepal-China communication links, on all levels.

It is believed that the Indian proxy population, in Nepal, supporting *Hindutva* politics, and the monarchy, have largely given the vote to the Left, which reflects a massive failure, of Indian diplomacy, in Nepal.

In the past, India had imposed an economic blockade, for 18 months, during the leadership of Rajiv Gandhi, after Nepal imported some weapons, from China.

The Indian-Nepalese relationship suffered a brunt recently when a new constitution was made in Nepal, that gave fewer powers to *Madheshi* ethnic group, living in the Terai region, who have a cultural affinity, with people of the Indian states of Uttar Pradesh, and Bihar.

With issues of citizenship, representation, inclusion, autonomy, and language remaining unaddressed, these problems, if not addressed, might lead to a political confrontation.

 In some pressure tactics, the *Madheshi* border had been closed, by its people, presumably, at the behest of New Delhi. At that moment in time, the Nepali Left had secured China's support, when the blockade lasted for six months.

India will try its best to renew diplomatic interests, as a 'big brother,' and will make sure that Nepal does not become an associate of Chinese state policy. Many Nepalese still look for jobs, in the plains of India, on a permanent, or seasonal basis.

As a neighbour, India also needs to make sure that Nepal does not play into the hands of 'red corridor' phenomenon, happening in India, which mainly consists of the insurgency of the *'Adivasis.'*

If we investigate the recent past, King Gyanendra, in 2005, facilitated China's entry, into the SAARC, as an observer country, even though member countries, endorsed the decision, unanimously.

Many political commentators have been critical of the PEON (Permanent Establishment of Nepal), where several advantageous minority castes, including Muslims, *Dalits, Janjatis* have resisted change, to its political, economic, and cultural power in the Nepali society.

This issue, having dogmatic factors, associated with it,

might keep the universal reform, attempted by political forces, in the country, in the backseat.

20 December, 2017

7

ELECTION UNREST IN HONDURAS

HONDURAS IS EXPERIENCING A STATE of great uncertainty after the 2017 November election.

The Honduran Electoral Supreme Tribunal (TSE), has examined the election result and has put the current President Juan Orlando Hernadez with a slight advantage over Salvador Nasralla.

To make matters worse, protestors have poured, onto the streets. They believe that the leftist opposition candidate, Salvador Nasralla, had won the election.

Amnesty International, the leading human rights group, has criticised the government, for using violence, and has expressed 'irregularities,' in the election.

It seems that things, in Honduras, are not blown out of proportions, and the tactics seem to be dangerous, and illegal. The opposition believes that over 5000 votes have not been counted, and considered.

Salvador Nasralla, a 64-year-old former TV presenter, with little political experience, claims to have proof of ballot fraud. He believes around 'one-third of ballot boxes have been tampered with. He demands that all ballot boxes be recounted, under the supervision of foreign observers.

In the recent unrest, security forces have extinguished

burning tires, that had been set across the capital, by protestors, backing Nasralla's Alliance Against Dictatorship Coalition.

Journalists had seen roadblocks, north, west, and south of this small Central American nation. In the southern province of Choluteca, there had been reports of soldiers, using live ammunition against a TV crew, but no one had been wounded.

Some hundred people had been arrested, in the first ten-day curfew, according to the Committee of Relatives, of the Detained-Disappeared, in Honduras (COFADEH). A 19-year-old woman was shot dead, and a football-loving kid, had been taken to a hospital, for surgery, after participating in protests.

Regional reporters claim that dozens of shops have been looted, and many buildings have been damaged. Queues of cars have rushed to petrol stations, to fill their car tanks, and shoppers have rushed to supermarkets, during the relaxation hours, before the curfew escalated.

The former president of the 'Alliance Against the Dictatorship Coalition,' Manuel Zelaya, an ally of the deceased Hugo Chavez, believes that it is the United States, that wants to impose Juan Orlando Hernandez, as the leader of the country.

Honduras is a major source of migrants, to the US, and it remains vulnerable, to its problems. This Central American nation has also been notorious, for cocaine trafficking routes, and is infamous for its gang culture, having the world's highest murder rate.

As half of the population in Honduras is already poor and

needs to find jobs, more chaos may slip the country, into some disaster.

In 2015, there were similar protests, in Honduras, against President Juan Orlando Hernandez, over an ongoing corruption scandal.

It was believed that through a government scheme, the president sucked millions of dollars, from the country's social security institution. About 3000 people were killed, for protesting the fraud.

The President, Juan Orlando has been accused of authoritarian rule, and for his neoliberal policies, over the years.

For this reason, the 2015 scandal erupted the *Indignados* movement, which organised 24 weeks of torch-lit marches, to demand an end to corruption, the creation of an independent anti-impunity commission, and the president's resignation. The movement's core demands remain unanswered.

Several of the banners read 'Out with narco-dictator JOH' in Spanish. The killing of the two police officers motivated the police to disobey orders, and crack down on protests harshly.
The Cobras, a special police force, that has received training, and funding, in the United States, as well as Tigres, another US trained elite police squad, recently gathered at headquarters, alongside rank-and-file members, of the transit police, border police, police investigations directorate, and preventative police, to engage collectively, in curbing down the mass dissent.

The Movement for Dignity and Justice (MADJ) allege

that security forces, including Cobras and military police, have engaged in illegal raids, as they showed up at MADJ property in the northern Atlantida department, looking for the group's general coordinator, Martín Fernandez, who has been illegally detained by police in the past and faces ongoing intimidation.

In 2009, Honduras experienced a US-backed coup, where the army ousted Manuel Zalaya.

The arrest of Mr Zelaya was the culmination of a battle, that had been simmering for weeks, over a referendum, that hoped to revise the Constitution. The US poured around $114 million in security aid into the country, despite a poor human right record. The aid, of about $17 million, also goes to Honduran security forces, for counter-narcotics and anti-gang programs, and to fund an effort to purge the police of corrupt officers and train recruits.

The coup paved the way for National Party Rule. It was believed that this coup was planned in Miami, at the Southern Command.

Many Hondurans, still express resentment, over this development, as militarisation has drastically increased, since the 2009 coup. It seems that there is a military dictatorship, going on in Honduras, in the guise of a democracy.

If the ballot boxes are re-examined, it could take some time, for the authorities, to compare thousands of ballot boxes, with the tally sheets.

Quite recently, United Nations Secretary-General, Antonio Guterres, had called on the Honduran government, 'to guarantee the rule of law,' and the 'protection of human rights,' within the country.

14 December, 2017

8

POLITICAL TRANSITION
IN ZIMBABWE

PRESIDENT ROBERT MUGABE, the self-styled 'grand old man' of Zimbabwe, was forced to resign, after 37 years, in power, in a November 2017 coup d'état, under pressure from the army, and the ruling ZANU-PF party.

As an incentive for his political retirement, he and his wife will receive millions of dollars, as a 'golden handshake'. He also has been granted immunity, from prosecution.

When a caravan of armour vehicles was spotted by journalists, two weeks back, in November 2017, it seemed that a coup against the former president was in the offing.

This nonagenarian leader, at 93, has been the longest-serving leader in Africa and is often called, Zimbabwe's Gaddafi.

He had been dismissed because he was believed to have led the collapse of the economy and instigating heightened repression, and poverty.

It also seemed, that his resignation, on public TV, was because of succumbing to pressure, pitted by some powerful, public organisations.

The head of the powerful organisation, of war veterans, accused the president, of being 'deaf and blind, to the wishes of the people'. Christopher Mutsvangwa, the former member of the ZANU PF party, had recently threatened, to 'call out the crowds again to do their business.'

Zimbabwean military had been angered about his latest move, towards ousting the former Vice President, Mugabe, whose supporters had been unhappy, about his dismissal.

The army wanted to fix the political situation, as they believed something bad was looming, in their government affairs. But many critics have accused the military, of taking the government down, for their benefits, which include rackets and money-seeking means.

When the new President Emerson Mnangagwa, was sworn, in November 2017, the opposition was unhappy about his comments, when he said that he regarded Mugabe, as his mentor.

'He led us in our struggle for national independence. He assumed responsibility for leadership, at a formative, and very challenging time,' Mnangagwa said, in his speech. 'To me personally, he remains a father, mentor, comrade in arms and my leader.'

At the same time, he had vowed, to end the policies, of the erstwhile ruler, and wanted to bring more jobs, to the country.

The opposition believes that this change of leadership is a choice, based on elitism, and not a people's revolution. They believe that Mnangagwa, as Mugabe's yes-man, will just keep the status quo, intact.

He also has been accused, of being an accomplice, with Mugabe, for the long-standing human rights abuses, in the country, in postcolonial Zimbabwe.

Western powers, such as Britain and the United States, were accused of keeping a wilful silence, to the perpetrated genocide.

It is believed by people that while working with Mugabe, Mnangagwa lead the feared Zimbabwean intelligence agency, as well as the defence, and justice ministries, and heightened state oppression, and brutality.

Most importantly, Mnangagwa has been tainted, by accusations of his involvement, in the Matabeleland massacres, in the 1980s, along with Mugabe.

In January 1983 Robert Mugabe's government launched a massive security clampdown, in Matabeleland. It was led by a North Korean-trained, almost exclusively *chiShona* - speaking army unit, known as the Fifth Brigade. They committed thousands of atrocities, including murders, gang rapes, and mass torture.

Mugabe's government called the operation '*Gukurahundi*'. In *chiShona* language, it was a metaphor for blood spilling violence, meaning 'for the rain that washes away the chaff (from the last harvest), before the spring rains.' It is estimated that between 10,000 to 20,000, unarmed civilians died, at the hands, of the Fifth Brigade.

At the current point in time, tens of thousands of people had gathered in Harare, in National Sports Stadium, cheering, dancing, and waving the national flags. These developments do reflect the optimism of the masses, as they see the former vice president sworn in, as their leader.

By getting stirred up by emotions through populism, it

is not rare to see people, cheering for leaders, who have accumulated political failures, and have blood on their hands.

In the past, Zimbabwe had been regarded as the 'breadbasket of Africa.' But, in Mugabe's time, the country suffered economic mismanagement, absenteeism, red tape, food shortages, and widespread corruption. His land reform programmes declined the agricultural output, especially, during the Fast Track Land Reform Programme, in 2001.

The production of staple food, such as wheat and maize, on average, never surpassed ten per cent. The unemployment rate has hovered, at around ninety percent. At this point, Mnangagwa, as a new leader, has promised to fight corruption, and bring back public funds, stashed in foreign banks, by individuals and companies.

In a Guardian article, correspondent Jason Burke wrote on November 18th, 2017: 'the only jobs are in government service, yet salaries are rarely paid. The best and the brightest have long fled abroad. Warehouses are empty, fields lie fallow. The busiest store in rural villages is the bottle shop, selling dirt-cheap spirits.'

In another article on 26th November 2017, he wrote: 'roads are rutted, many rural communities have no electricity, education is basic and healthcare almost non-existent. A life expectancy of 60 is one of the lowest in the world.'

In an important development, Zimbabwean activist pastor, Evan Mawarire has been acquitted by the court, for trying to overthrow former president Robert Mugabe, in protests in 2016, that shut down major cities and paralysed public transport.

The judge made Mawarire, free of charges because he had called for non-violent protests, in response to the country's economic crisis, in 2016.

On social media, such as Twitter, users used slogans, such as #FreshStart, and #NewZimbabwe, to register their protests.

29 November, 2017

9

LEBANON IS PLAGUED WITH SAUDI INTERESTS

SAUDI ARABIA HAS BEEN ACCUSED, of playing a political game, in Lebanon. Crown Prince Mohammad bin Salman's role is believed to have been plausible, in the recent resignation of Lebanese Prime Minister, Saad Hariri, in a televised speech in November 2017, while Hariri toured Saudi Arabia. Iran calls it a 'rare form,' of foreign intervention.

Riyadh, somehow, happens to be perturbed, about the current Lebanese crises, mostly because they enjoy an influence, in the *Sunni* Lebanese community.

Saad Hariri is believed to have announced his resignation, to safeguard any threats, against his life. He had been fearful that he might suffer the same fate as his father, Rafiq Hariri, who died in a car bomb, believed to have been carried out by Shi'ite extremists, in 2005. Although, the interior minister, and the security forces, are affirming that they are not aware of any such threats, issued against Saad Hariri.

Lebanon has had a long history, of being a proxy for Saudi political influences, and for the Iranians, post-Islamic Revolution in 1979.

It has been believed that *Hezbollah* was formed on the insistence of Iran, to tackle Israeli occupation, of the Lebanese territory. The stances of *Hezbollah* have made them a target of Saudis, who in many ways, are helping to extend the Israeli, and US foreign policy, on Lebanese soil.

In many of Saad Hariri's former speeches, he spoke against Iranian interests. His past speeches have been regarded as surrogate examples of Saudi politics. These realities have directly instigated *Hezbollah*, who are strong in the country's south, enjoying power at certain levels, in the government, military and bureaucracy.

The Kingdom has followed an expansionist approach, in war zones, including Syria, Yemen, and a stern resistance, of a recent trade embargo, against Qatar. But now, the country has been facing several internal and external pressures, at a tumultuous time of proxy wars, which has made the whole Middle East a new ground, for an international conflict.

Saudis want to push the regional balance of power, towards them. They think that the current geopolitical scenario is strengthening Syrian President Bashar Al Assad, and his allies, like Iran, and the regional rival, Hezbollah. So, they are seeking means to strengthen their dominance, including in the Levant.

Saudi Arabia, by every means, wants to be a pivotal force, in the Middle East, by aiding individuals and groups, who want to get aligned, with their political postures. Lebanon happens to be one such place, where its former prime ministers have made fortunes, by just aligning themselves with the Saudis. Some of them even went to have dual nationalities.

Saad Hariri, himself, has been involved in his high-profile family-owned construction business, dating back to 1970, which he closed, just a year, earlier. Nevertheless, the stock of money, which Hariri has left in Saudi Arabia, puts him under the leverage of Saudi interests, including political.

In history, Riyadh has gone further, in cementing relationships, not only with finances but also by offering marriages, with senior Saudi princes, in Lebanon's *Sunni*-dominated political lobby. The main goal had been to neutralise nationalist, and leftist threats, coming from Beirut, by using the *Sunni* Lebanese leaders, for their aims.

In a recent press report, the desperation of Houthi rebels was noted when they fired a long-range missile, aimed at Riyadh International Airport, a day before Saad Hariri's resignation, who is himself, a dual Saudi-Lebanese national.

Saudis called the airport attack attempt 'a plot,' led by Iran. The ruling of the Crown Prince, to convict the remaining political dissidents, in his country, was followed by this attack. This event had been camouflaged by Kingdom's 'anti-corruption purge.'

There is something about Lebanon's political ethos. The quagmire runs deep. It is a country where Christians and Muslims live together but still have failed to realise a common vision, for their homeland. The answer to this problem lies in sectarian interests, often distinguished by ethnic and religious lines. Much of it has been credited to the Taif agreement drafted in 1989.

In the Senate, Christians and Muslims share equal power. Under the ruling 'troika,' the president must be a Maronite Christian, the speaker of the parliament a *Shi'ite* Muslim, and the prime minister, a *Sunni* Muslim.

In the streets of Lebanon, montages of Saudi kings have been seen in *Sunni* neighbourhoods, just like montages of

Khomeini, Khamenei, and other Iranian political figures, that are decorated, in *Shi'ite* neighbourhoods.

It seems that the bitterness, between Beirut and Riyadh, has escalated, to a new level. Saudis, along with Kuwaitis, and Emiratis, are insisting that Lebanese nationals, leave their country. This has happened four times, in five years. Iranians, on the other hand, have been loathing the Saudis, just because of their cordial relationship, with the Israelis.

As Lebanon's relationship with France, goes back to colonial times, analysts are keeping their fingers crossed, about the outcome of Macron's recent visit, to Riyadh, which may have ameliorated tensions.

If any sort of conventional war happens, this fragile peace, in the Levant, will be blown to smithereens, involving Palestinian and Syrian refugees, producing a new refugee problem, on the radar, towards the shores of Europe.

15 November, 2017

10

POLITICAL UPHEAVALS IN LIBYA

SAIF AL ISLAM, LATE MUAMMAR GADDAFI'S son, has re-emerged in the Libyan political scene that appears fractured. A militia group based, in the Libyan city of Zintan, has set him free, since June 2017.

Saif al Islam had been released under 'General Amnesty Law,' passed by the Libyan House of Representatives. Now, it will be crucial to ponder, on his intents: he wants to initiate a peace mission, but international law has a different story to tell, about his past political actions.

In 2011, he quelled a rebellion, against the ruling regime of his father. Before the 2011 civil war, he was believed to be a moderate, unlike his deceased father.

A court in Tripoli has sentenced him to death, in absentia, two years back. He had been facing an arrest warrant from International Criminal Court, for 'crimes against humanity,' at the time of his capture, in November 2011.

But the Libyan government filed an appeal, on this decision, stating that Saif al Islam should be tried, at home. His legal case has become a matter of national importance, in Libya. Contrarily, Human Rights Watch believes that Saif al Islam's defence trial was not presented fairly, by his attorney.

At his return to politics, Libya is going through a chaotic phase. The government does not have a unified code of conduct. There is a Tripoli-based National Accord Government (GNA), and the Tobruk-based House of Representatives (HoR). The HoR have their loyalty to the Libyan National Army, under General Khalifa Haftar.

In 2016, the Libyan National Army, winning the support of local tribes, and gaining strides, in and around Benghazi, was involved, in instigating rifts, between the rival government factions, and seized oil ports, namely Es Sider, Ras Lanuf, Brega and Zueitina. These ports, previously under Petrol Facilities Guard, had made a pact with GNA, to end a three-year economic blockade.

Islamic State attacked the oil ports, of Raus Lanuf and Es Sider, in 2016. Since then, Benghazi Defence Brigades, are also attacking Libyan National Army posts.

Western governments back GNA, but General Haftar, who controls eastern Libya, is supported by Egypt and UAE for his anti - Islamic State standpoint. He has also been tainted as an agent of the erstwhile Gaddafi regime, and a divisive figure, who is hell-bent to establish a military dictatorship. His stances have also prolonged the conflict in Libya.

In December 2015, the UN brokered a Libyan Peace Agreement (LPA), where it was decided that Presidential Council will preside, over the GNA.

However, it became mandatory for Tripoli-based GNA, to be endorsed by the Tobruk-based House of Representatives (HoR).

However, on two occasions, the HoR turned down the list of GNA ministers, and they also want the current Presidential Council, to be dissolved.

Regional analysts believe as long there is a rift between the governing entities, the Islamic State will take full advantage of this divide.

At the present, there are 'city-states,' that are scrambling for power, in western and southern Libya. There is also the dominance of tribes, in central and eastern Libya.

Most of the Libyan masses seem to have varying loyalties. It also indicates as if multiple governments are running in Libya, not one. How will Saif al Islam change that? It remains to be seen.

Libyan Central Bank, which oversees the oil business, enjoys a lukewarm relationship, with the Presidential Council. Statistics suggest that the armed conflict, and political disputes, have reduced Libya's oil production, to about 200,000 barrels, per day (bpd), from the 1.6 million (bpd).

The Libyan government believes that the Islamic State is regrouping, after their fallout, in 2015-2016.

Many of the recruits are coming from Syria and Iraq, escaping the air raids, from the Russians, and the Americans.

Under the Trump administration, 'precision air strikes,' against the Islamic State, have regained their course. It seems that only a stronger military apparatus can defeat the Islamic State.

Post-Gaddafi era, thousands of rebel fighters had stormed through the city of Sirte, and operated in 'small cells.'

When Islamic State launched a suicide attack, in Misrata, it was believed to be a revenge killing, against the killing of militias, from Misrata, where the government forces had intent, to wipe out rebels, from Sirte.

The government, to get hold of the situation, has compiled a report, on the cause of extremism in Libya. It is also raising the bar of its international diplomacy, to pacify internal threats. The government also ordered arrest warrants, for around 800 militias, lately.

Libyans, over time, have expected nothing from the peace talks. At this moment, it will be interesting to see what kind of role Saif al Islam will play.

Does he have the charisma left to start a political settlement?

It seems that he has long lost power, and the trust of his people. As a leader, can he unite his country, when he presumably has blood on his hands?

Varying political sentiments make perplexing conclusions. Many Libyans think that the noose should hold him, while there is a parallel faction that believes he can regain the support of common Libyans, and get them out of dubious forces. The coming time will be the biggest test for Libya.

24 October, 2017

11

SOUTH CHINA SEA DISPUTE

With OVER $5 TRILLION OF TRADE, passing through the South China Sea, the strategic importance of this sea route continues to dominate.

Any political volatility would not only harm the countries, in a territorial dispute, but also larger trading economies, in the area, like Japan, and South Korea.

It is a place where all global trade converges. South China Sea dispute is not only about oil, and natural gas, but also about enormous fishing reserves.

International media has mostly given attention, to this trade route, when any natural catastrophe has occurred.

In its quest for naval expansion and defence, the Chinese State has already deployed more SSN nuclear submarines, and SSBN ballistic missile submarines, in the region, from Qindao in the north, across the Yellow Sea, from South Korea, to Yulin, on Hainan Island, in heart of South China Sea.

It seems that China wants to exert its authoritarian control, over the sea, in the recent past, even though it ratified the Land of the Sea treaty, in 1996.

Chinese state has even built elaborate signal stations, especially near Hainan. It also indicates that China is trying to pull the economic competition, in the South

China Sea towards itself, with the help of its military, just like the US dominated the Caribbean, in the 19ᵗʰ century.

It regards South China Sea, as its own 'continental shelf,' and cites historical records of *Han's Dynasty* discovery, and *Ming Qing* dynasty control, of the Paracel Island (also claimed by Taiwan and Vietnam), and Spratly Island (also claimed by Philippines, Taiwan, Vietnam, and Malaysia), to back their claims, reflecting a Middle Kingdom mentality.

Even other countries, that have been affected, by the dispute, in these troubled waters, like Indonesia, Malaysia, and Singapore, have increased their arms imports, considerably. All these developments reflect a complex geo-politics structure.

Although, the Chinese have pacified two hundred areas of dispute, with Vietnam, during the eight-year negotiation, in the 1990s, with demarcation work, completed, in 2008.

Vietnam's GDP heavily relies on maritime trade, and it claims a line two hundred miles, straight out, into the South China Sea, which Vietnamese call the 'East Sea'. This complies, with the Conventions of the Law of the Sea, but it strangely overlaps with maritime areas, claimed by China, Malaysia, Cambodia, and Thailand, in the adjacent Gulf of Thailand.

Chinese even claim that they have settled the maritime dispute, with Vietnam, in the Gulf of Tonkin (where the northern Vietnamese coastline is blocked by open sea by China's Hainan Island), by dividing the energy-rich gulf into half, although the mouth of the gulf still needs to be demarcated. But logically, this gulf remains a disputed area.

As the United States guards all the sea lines of communication, necessary for international trade, many analysts, opposing Chinese dominance, believe that, the United States, with its sturdy air and naval power, can play a role in balancing power, in the South China Sea. Importantly, it can likely limit China, to its maps.

At the present, the Philippines dominate the eastern edge of South China Sea, Vietnam dominates the western edge, and the Chinese dominate the northern edge.

According to scholar, Clive Schofield, Vietnam is a 'principal protagonist,' in the South China Sea. He believes that Indonesia already has a well-defined foreign policy, on the issue of the South China Sea, whereas Malaysia prefers to be low-key, politically. Although, he also notes that the Philippines still has a few cards to play politically, and ascertains that Brunei has already solved the problem, with China.

Pratas Island, controlled by Taiwan, has been declared as their national park. In history, the Taiwanese controlled the island, for harvesting abundant fish stocks. Taiwanese coastal guards still expcl Chinese and Vietnamese fishing boats. Currently, Taiwan faces a threat of 'Finlandisation' by China.

The Philippines archipelago, which calls the South China Sea, as 'West Philippine Sea,' must address several internal problems. It imports all its oil, by sea. Any instability will lead the archipelago nation, to lose access to hydrocarbon reserves, in areas of Spratly Island, and Scarborough Shoal, as well as loss of existing fisheries.

Infact, the recent rift between China and the Philippines, in Scarborough Shoal, in the spring of 2012, 120 miles west of Luzon, showed that the Chinese had the intent of policing the waters, with its dispatch of 20 lightly armed maritime vessels.

It seems that the Philippine archipelago has no choice, but to ask for the patronage of the United States, because it is vulnerable to military attacks. It may also become 'Finlandised' by China.

Historically, Washington sent aid to the Philippines ($200 million every year), when Clark and Subic bases, were still operational there.

China did not allow the Philippines to explore fifteen blocks, because it fell with China's 'nine-dashed line' (that encircles 90 per cent of contested waters by China on the sea map). In fact, US foreign policy officials, believe, that China is looking for a 'dry patch of land,' in the area, for naval expansion.

Philippines has also contested, this international dispute, in the Court of Arbitration, in the Hague, as Manila argues that this 'nine-dashed line,' exceeds the limits of maritime entitlements, under the UN convention, on the Law of the Sea (UNCLOS).

22 October, 2017

12

ITALY'S FIGHT AGAINST ISLAMIC EXTREMISM

WHEN ISLAMIC EXTREMISM SPLIT OVER to Europe, after the 9/11 attacks, the Islamic war had truly become global. Britain, France, Germany, and Spain were attacked mercilessly, and randomly. But, Italy, has all along avoided the Islamic war, on its soil.

However, the rising threats of Islamic war that Italy can face, in future, can no longer be undermined.

In August 2017, when a video was circulated, by al-Hayat, a pro-ISIS organisation, based in the war-ravaged city, of Marawi, Philippines, the ISIS sympathisers threatened the Vatican, and Rome, while tearing the image of Pope Francis, in a sacked Roman Catholic Church.

The video had been directed towards jihadi sympathisers based, in Italy, that showed militants wrecking statues of Jesus, Mary, St. Joseph, and ripping pictures of Pope Francis, and Pope Benedict XVI.

A graphic illustration of a young man, holding a knife, with the Italian phrase, *'Devi Combatterli,'* meaning, 'You must fight them,' was also circulated on Telegram, the most preferred social app of Islamic militants.

The montage was then reproduced by the US-based Site

Intelligence Group, and then by the mainstream media, such as Fox News, lately. These developments have become concerning to Italian security agencies.

Italy has accounted for about eighty-two per cent of unauthorised arrivals, in 2017 alone, mostly through the central Mediterranean route, ending at Lampedusa Island, in Sicily.

Therefore, it seems that even if migrants are not treated as criminals, the argument of a link between extremism, and immigration cannot be largely undermined.

According to inputs from the Italian Interior Ministry, up to seventy suspected Islamic extremists, were deported from Italy, in 2017.

It also appears that Italian authorities have decided to take a hard-line approach. Counterterrorism authorities have questioned about 160,593 people, between March 2016 and March 2017. They have interrogated about 34,000 people, at airports.

More than 500 websites have been shut down, and nearly half a million websites are monitored. Even *Lega Nord* party members have asked the local mosque preachers, to give sermons in Italian.

On 19th August 2017, three extremist Moroccan Muslims, were sent back to Syria. A month after on 24th September, when a Boeing 737 took off from Bologna airport, bound for Tirana, Albania's capital, it carried the 209th expelled person, from Italy, since 2015, after being under constant police scrutiny. The 22-year-old Muslim had been arrested, for trying to persuade the worshippers, not to enter a church.

Defence Minister Roberta Pinotti, in 2015, commented that 87 Islamic fighters travelled through Italy, where only 12 had Italian passports.

Italian law enforcement agencies, however, often concede that they have fewer suspects to monitor, than their French and British counterparts. They believe Italy's second-generation Muslims, which are only a small number (0.3% of Italian residents) are susceptible to radicalisation (against 3% in Britain and 3.9% in France).

Apart from that, Italy has no Muslim ghettos, like the French *'banlieues.'* The predominance, of small and medium towns, has also made it easier to monitor the situation.

Arturo Varvelli, of the Milan-based Institute for International Political Studies, believes that the Italian mafia (the Camorra around Naples, the Cosa Nostra in Sicily, and Ndrangheta in Calabria), dominant in Italy's south, has averted the jihadis, in making a stronghold, in the country.

Italian law officials also believe that the wealth of experience, that they have acquired over the years, to fight against Italian organised mafia, that ran amok, during the 1970s and 1980s, has given them the advantage to guard the system. It has helped them in understanding the importance of increased cooperation, between the police and the intelligence.

Issuing wiretap orders, holding suspects without charge for up to four days, hiring informants, and electronic surveillance, has been encouraged by judges, and the police, to tackle extremism threats, a stance that is like what they did, during the 'Years of Lead,' of the mafia.

In the past, Italy suffered at the hands, of its own people. Factually, the 1969 Piazza Fontana bombing, the 1974 Piazza della Loggia bombing, and 1980 Bologna bombing, were some major attacks carried out by local far-right groups, like Ordine Nuovo, whereas countless assassinations, drug and weapons trafficking, waste mismanagement, conspiracies, and extortions, perpetuated by the mafia, have harmed the social fabric, in Italy.

Michele Groppi, who teaches at the Defence Academy, of the UK, points out another important factor, where he believes that jihadists have used Italy, as a 'logistical base' to Europe, and that is what kept the country safe.

Despite this, several high-profile jihadis have attained notoriety, such as Youssef Zaghba, a Moroccan-born Italian, one of the three extremists, who used a truck, and some knives to kill eight people, on and around London Bridge, on 3rd June 2017.

Many recent attacks in Europe have had some sort of Italian connection. Anis Amri, the Tunisian who attacked a Berlin Christmas market in 2016, was shot on the outskirts of Milan by Italian security officials. He was believed to have been radicalised, in a prison, in Sicily. Mohammad Lahouaiej Bouhlel, a Tunisian behind the deadly attack in Nice, France, in 2016, was identified by Italian police, as having spent time, in the border town of Ventimiglia, in Liguria.

Michele Groppi also believes, that if the war in Libya intensifies, it will be a very sensitive matter, because major Italian cities may become the next target of the jihadist insurgency.

21 October, 2017

13

ANGELA MERKEL'S GLOBAL ACCEPTANCE

ANGELA MERKEL'S ACHIEVEMENT in winning four consecutive federal elections in Germany was remarkable by any democratic standard. Few leaders in modern Europe have managed such longevity in office. Yet remaining in power for so long should not be confused with unqualified success or ideological clarity. Merkel's leadership was defined less by sweeping vision than by caution, pragmatism, and an ability to endure crises without fully owning their long-term consequences. Her strength lay in survival rather than transformation, and this distinction is crucial to any serious assessment of her legacy.

Internationally, Merkel was often portrayed as a moral counterweight to the rise of authoritarian leaders. In the Anglo-American press she was frequently described as a stabilising figure and, following the election of Donald Trump in 2016, was often characterised as a potential 'leader of the free world'—a label she herself never embraced. The phrase reflected both her authority and her discomfort with global leadership. Yet this reluctance often translated into delayed decisions and strategic ambiguity, particularly during the eurozone crisis, the migration influx, and Germany's dealings with Russia. Merkel was admired for her steadiness, but her hesitations often left Europe waiting for clarity at critical moments.

Merkel assumed office in 2005 just before the global economic order entered its most turbulent phase. The 2008 financial crash and the subsequent eurozone debt crisis tested not only Germany's economic resilience but also the foundations of European integration. Her most cited accomplishment—preventing the euro from collapsing—came with serious costs. During the Greek debt crisis, Germany emerged as the principal advocate of fiscal discipline and austerity measures attached to bailout programmes, placing budgetary restraint above expansive social spending in countries such as Greece, Spain, and Portugal. The human cost of these policies was widely debated. Paul Krugman, writing in The New York Times, criticised Merkel's economic approach for deepening recessions and prolonging hardship in southern Europe. Unlike the United States, which responded to crisis through stimulus and monetary expansion, Germany prioritised spending cuts, and balanced budgets. While this reassured German voters, it generated resentment across much of Europe, where Merkel's leadership was increasingly seen as rigid, technocratic, and indifferent to inequality.

Domestically, Merkel's electoral success owed much to her ideological adaptability. She steadily absorbed policies traditionally associated with her opponents—introducing a minimum wage, exiting nuclear power, and relaxing her party's stance on social issues. Several German commentators and political scientists argued that this strategy weakened traditional ideological distinctions and contributed to broader changes in Germany's party system. The rise of the far-right Alternative für Deutschland (AfD) cannot be separated from this long-term erosion of political contestation. Merkel's pragmatism kept her in power, but it also hollowed out the ideological clarity of mainstream politics.

The 2015 migration crisis marked the most divisive moment of Merkel's chancellorship. Her declaration—

'Wir schaffen das' ('We can manage this')—was praised by The Washington Post as a rare expression of moral leadership in Europe. Yet moral clarity was not matched by institutional preparedness. Local authorities faced significant challenges in housing, integrating, and providing services for large numbers of asylum seekers, contributing to political controversy over migration policy. The backlash strengthened nationalist forces and reshaped German and European politics. Merkel's stance was courageous, but the lack of planning undermined its effectiveness and fuelled polarisation.

Her foreign policy reputation as a stabiliser also deserves closer scrutiny. In 2008 she refused to grant Georgia a NATO Membership Action Plan, despite pressure from Washington. Some Western analysts viewed the move as pragmatic diplomacy designed to avoid provoking Russia. Yet, in hindsight, critics questioned whether such restraint encouraged Russian assertiveness, particularly after events in Crimea and eastern Ukraine. Her relationship with Russia was marked by similar contradictions. Merkel supported EU sanctions following the annexation of Crimea, yet also backed the Nord Stream 2 gas pipeline.

The project was criticised by numerous Eastern European governments, EU officials, and energy-security analysts who argued it increased European dependence on Russian gas and weakened broader European energy security. Merkel's belief that economic interdependence could moderate geopolitical conflict appeared increasingly outdated in a more confrontational global environment.

Merkel remained a committed supporter of European integration, but her vision of Europe was limited. She favoured fiscal rules, economic supervision, and structural reforms, while resisting deeper political union that might have required Germany to shoulder greater redistributive responsibilities. Critics argued that her conception of Europe emphasised discipline and stability more than solidarity and shared political risk. Merkel's Europe was functional, but it lacked the ambition to build a truly united political community.

Her domestic reforms were equally complex. The decision to phase out nuclear power after the Fukushima disaster was widely praised, yet The Wall Street Journal and numerous German energy analysts pointed to unintended consequences: higher electricity prices, greater reliance on fossil fuels during parts of the energy transition, and increased dependence on imported natural gas, including supplies from Russia. The abolition of military conscription was framed as progressive, but defence analysts writing in Frankfurter Allgemeine Zeitung later criticised Germany's weakened military readiness within NATO. Merkel's reforms often carried hidden costs that became apparent only later.

International recognition followed Merkel throughout her career. She topped Forbes' list of the world's most powerful women multiple times, was named TIME's Person of the Year in 2015, and received the Charlemagne Prize for European unity. Yet such accolades did not end debate over the effectiveness of her leadership or the long-term consequences of her policies. As Martin Wolf argued in the Financial Times, Merkel excelled at crisis management and incremental problem-solving—skills that proved valuable in turbulent times but were less effective in addressing deeper structural challenges.

Merkel's political temperament was deeply shaped by her upbringing in East Germany. Living under a surveillance state taught her caution, respect for limits, and a strong sense of restraint. She governed by defining boundaries rather than offering grand narratives. This background explains her preference for pragmatism over vision, and her tendency to avoid bold ideological commitments. Merkel was not a leader of sweeping reforms, but of careful adjustments and incremental survival.

In the end, Angela Merkel was neither a heroic saviour of liberal democracy nor merely a caretaker of the status quo. She was a crisis manager whose authority rested on patience rather than passion, and survival rather than vision. Her legacy is best understood not through admiration alone, but through the unresolved questions her leadership leaves behind—about Europe's cohesion, Germany's responsibility, and the long-term cost of stability without transformation. Merkel's career demonstrates the power of endurance in politics. She held office longer than most of her contemporaries, navigated crises that could have broken weaker leaders, and maintained Germany's position as Europe's anchor. Yet her reluctance to embrace deeper reforms or articulate a clear vision means her legacy is defined as much by what she avoided as by what she achieved. The unresolved tensions of her era—between austerity and solidarity, openness and security, pragmatism and ambition—remain challenges for Germany and Europe today.

14 October, 2017

14

DUTERTE'S MARTIAL LAW

PRESIDENT OF PHILIPPINES, RODRIGO DUTERTE has extended martial law, in the southern part of his country, until 31st December 2017.

He thinks that the red brigade of communists, and the liberals, are making conspiracies, to oust him, who have a stronghold, in the south of the country.

More importantly, to tackle the rise of the Islamic State there, he has made his political intentions even clearer. Although, several unhappy Filipinos have recently burned several of his effigies in Manila, near the Mendiola Bridge.

The protestors likened him to 'Hitler,' 'Marcos' and a 'lapdog of US imperialism.'

It had been a couple of his close military associates, who had advised him, to impose martial law, in the southern Philippines.

In several of his public declarations, he had vowed to end this martial law, after the end of fighting in Marawi, located in Mindanao, the second largest island of the Philippines.

Marawi is a densely populated city and has become an easy breeding place, for the Islamic State rebels, to nurture their militant activities. The city belongs to a region, with a nearly four-hundred-year war history.

Logically, it is always hard to limit causalities, when forces are on the prowl, for an operation clean up. It has been five months, since the Battle of Marawi started, in May 2017.

Foreign countries, such as Australia, China, and the United States, and internal non-state groups, such as the Moro National Liberation Front, have allied together, to counter the militant activities, of the Islamic State, in Mindanao. Militants have burned up a church, a central jail, and schools. Over 200,000 people have been displaced.

Although Duterte claims that the Battle of Marawi, is in its final phase, many political commentators have claimed that the Armed Forces have been struggling, in the battle. A weak rule of law and poverty has heightened political tensions, in the territory.

The Muslims of Southern Philippines *(Moro)* largely belong to the tribe of *Tausug (Suluk)*, who fought the Spanish colonial rule, and four decades of American colonialism, through the Moro Rebellion (1899-1903), until the independence of the Philippines, in 1946.

Coming back to the time, several places, like the Bato Ali Mosque and the Jamiatu Marawi Al-Islamia Foundation, have now been used, by the Muslim gunmen, as their command centre.

Throughout history, Muslims in the Philippines, have believed that Christian Filipinos have been unjustly using their land, with the government's resettlement policy. The conflict between these groups has cost about 120,000 lives, over four decades.

At the moment, the AFP remains one of the weakest forces in the region. Out of 130,000 army personnel, only a handfuls are operational. This issue is the government's new challenge, especially at the time of martial law.

The country now spends only 1 per cent of its GDP, on its defence. Add to that, the money spent on the recent operations has cost them around 2.5- 3 billion pesos.

Several challenges, such as rebalancing troops, need to be addressed, and budgetary allocations for military training, as per inputs given by government spokespersons. For this, a military modernisation plan, from 2017 to 2028, has also been chalked out.

To buy certain military gear like helmets, vests, night vision goggles, and ammunition, money has been drawn from several long-term ongoing projects.

The inclusion of drones and facial recognition technology has been under Duterte's plans, but many of his advisors believe that the Philippines needs to improve its intelligence, surveillance, and reconnaissance capabilities (ISR in short). Hence, how things will improve from the political-legislative side, needs to be watched closely.

The aim of Islamic State, in the Philippines, had been launched with the Maute Group, a Salafi jihadist group that established a stronghold, in the province of Lanao Del Saur, in Mindanao, in February 2016.

After the 2016 Davao City bombing, the Philippines government, and its intelligence services have started to take tough measures, to tackle the Islamic State insurgency.

Recently, Duterte also made reports of sieging surrounding

cities of Marawi, in Mindanao, which could come under assault as well.

All these developments testify that Duterte is seriously seeking, to neutralise internal threats, in the country. That is why a potent military strategy, under Duterte's regime, is coming up.

He has already allocated a lucrative amount of budget, as a military fund, a plan like his predecessor, Benigno Aquino III.

In the past, several groups like Abu Sayyaf have pleaded allegiance, to the Islamic State. Several of its members, convicted for attacks in the country, have had links with Maute Group. These developments highly indicate the rising threats the Philippines is facing, from Islamic insurgency.

Going back to history, when the 'Jabidah massacre' had been done by the Philippine Armed Forces, in 1968, the Moro Liberation Front launched militant activities, to achieve their goals of autonomy, in the southern Philippines.

It was Muammar Gaddafi, who brokered a deal between the Philippine government, and the erstwhile Moro Liberation Front leaders, for autonomy, in the Mindanao region. But, after the eventual breakup of the party (Moro National Liberation Front and Moro Islamic Liberation Front), Moro Islamic Liberation Front, historically, continued to resist their armed struggle, until a series of negotiations in 2008, and a significant truce deal, in 2012.

Recently, about forty bodies, buried in a mass grave, had been retrieved in Marawi. It just gives some of the impressions, of this war-torn city, in the southern Philippines, where the Muslim militants kept around 300 people hostages.

9 October, 2017

15

POLITICAL REPRESSION
IN CAMBODIA

As THE 2026 GENERAL ELECTION APPROACHED in Cambodia, concerns over political openness intensified. Critics of Prime Minister Hun Sen and the Cambodian People's Party (CPP) argued that the electoral environment had become increasingly restrictive, with authority concentrated around the executive and growing influence exerted over key state institutions, including the judiciary, security apparatus and media. These concerns were not merely rhetorical. The closure of The Cambodia Daily in September 2017, the expulsion of the United States-based National Democratic Institute (NDI), and sustained pressure on independent radio stations broadcasting Radio Free Asia and Voice of America programming were widely documented by international observers as evidence of a broader contraction of civic space. Human Rights Watch, Amnesty International and Reporters Without Borders all reported a sustained pattern of legal and administrative pressure directed at independent journalists, trade unions, civil society organisations, and opposition-linked groups in the run-up to the election.

This political consolidation unfolded alongside significant economic transformation. Over the past two decades, Cambodia has achieved substantial reductions in poverty, driven largely by labour-intensive export growth, particularly in the garment sector, alongside expansion in agriculture, construction, and tourism. Assessments by the World Bank and the Asian Development Bank confirm sustained improvements in living standards since the early 2000s, while also highlighting persistent structural vulnerabilities. A considerable proportion of the population remains only marginally above the poverty line, leaving many households highly susceptible to commodity price volatility, climate-related shocks, and insecure employment. High energy costs, infrastructure deficits, and limited industrial diversification continue to constrain long-term economic development. Cambodia's export-oriented economy also remains heavily dependent on preferential access to Western markets, rendering it sensitive to changes in international trade policy and intensifying regional competition.

These economic gains have not translated into evenly distributed social protection. Labour rights organisations, including the International Labour Organisation (ILO), Better Factories Cambodia, Human Rights Watch, Amnesty International, the Clean Clothes Campaign and domestic trade unions such as the Cambodian Labour Confederation (CLC) and the Coalition of Cambodian Apparel Workers' Democratic Union (C.CAWDU), have repeatedly documented wages that remain insufficient relative to living costs, excessive overtime, inconsistent enforcement of labour standards and restrictions on collective bargaining. Although a statutory minimum wage exists for garment workers, enforcement gaps and the widespread use of short-term contracts continue to weaken workers' bargaining power.

Factory conditions illustrate these structural pressures. Reporting by the ILO, Better Factories Cambodia and non-governmental organisations has documented recurring incidents of heat stress, fatigue associated with prolonged working hours, dehydration and inadequate nutrition, all of which have contributed to repeated mass fainting episodes in garment factories. Government agencies and humanitarian organisations have also highlighted flooding in industrial zones as an increasing risk to electrical safety in factories and workers' accommodation. Together, these conditions have contributed to sustained labour migration, particularly to Thailand, as many workers seek more secure and better-paid employment opportunities beyond Cambodia's industrial centres.

Land governance has further compounded rural vulnerability. Human rights organisations, including LICADHO and Amnesty International, have documented the expansion of economic land concessions associated with displacement, deforestation and the erosion of subsistence agriculture. Illegal logging has likewise been widely reported by environmental monitoring organisations, contributing to long-term ecological degradation and undermining rural livelihoods. Collectively, these pressures have accelerated both rural-to-urban and cross-border migration, particularly among younger workers entering increasingly precarious labour markets.

Earlier labour unrest, especially the large-scale protests in Phnom Penh during 2013–2014, reflected deeper structural tensions surrounding wages, inequality, and political representation. These demonstrations were met through a combination of negotiation and forceful repression, underscoring the limited scope for independent labour mobilisation. While trade unions continue to operate formally, both domestic and international observers have consistently argued that their autonomy remains constrained in practice by legal ambiguity, administrative restrictions, and political pressure.

These contemporary developments are inseparable from Cambodia's Cold War history, although they should be understood within the framework of established historical scholarship rather than speculative interpretation. Cambodia became deeply entangled in the geopolitical rivalries of the Vietnam War, despite Prince Norodom Sihanouk's policy of formal neutrality. From 1969 to 1973, the United States conducted extensive aerial bombing campaigns over eastern Cambodia, initially through the secret Operation Menu and subsequently under the broader Operation Freedom Deal, targeting North Vietnamese and Viet Cong sanctuaries operating inside Cambodian territory. More than half a million tonnes of bombs were dropped, causing widespread destruction, displacement, and civilian casualties. While historians continue to debate the extent of its political impact, scholars including Ben Kiernan and Taylor Owen argue that the bombing contributed to rural radicalisation and created conditions that the Khmer Rouge later exploited for recruitment, whereas David P. Chandler emphasises that the movement's rise also reflected domestic political instability, Prince Sihanouk's endorsement of the insurgency following his overthrow, North Vietnamese support and the weaknesses of the Lon Nol government.

The Khmer Rouge regime (1975–1979), led by Pol Pot, was responsible for one of the twentieth century's most devastating episodes of mass violence. Scholarly estimates place the number of deaths resulting from executions, forced labour, starvation and disease at approximately 1.5 to 2 million people. The regime's programme of radical social engineering included the forced evacuation of urban populations, the abolition of markets and currency, agricultural collectivisation and mass executions at sites such as Tuol Sleng prison. Forced collectivisation, excessive rice procurement, unrealistic production targets, forced labour, disease and widespread starvation together produced one of the worst humanitarian catastrophes of the modern era.

Relations with neighbouring Vietnam deteriorated into armed conflict, culminating in cross-border atrocities including the Ba Chúc massacre of 1978, during which Khmer Rouge forces killed large numbers of Vietnamese civilians. The regime was ultimately overthrown in January 1979 following Vietnam's military intervention, which established the People's Republic of Kampuchea. Rather than bringing an immediate end to the conflict, however, the intervention internationalised Cambodia's crisis within the wider geopolitical context of the Cold War.

Following the regime's overthrow, China became the Khmer Rouge's principal external patron, providing military, logistical and diplomatic support as part of its broader strategic rivalry with Vietnam after the Sino-Vietnamese War of 1979. This interpretation is firmly established in the scholarship of Ben Kiernan and David P. Chandler, both of whom situate Cambodia within the wider dynamics of Cold War proxy conflict in Southeast Asia. During the same period, Thailand assumed an important logistical role by serving as a rear base for several Cambodian resistance factions operating along the Thai-Cambodian border.

The United States neither supported the Khmer Rouge government during its rule nor exercised operational control over its military forces. Nevertheless, American policy during the 1980s formed part of a broader strategy of containing Vietnamese and Soviet influence in Southeast Asia. Within this geopolitical context, diplomatic arrangements enabled the Coalition Government of

Democratic Kampuchea—which included Khmer Rouge representatives alongside non-communist resistance factions—to retain Cambodia's seat at the United Nations throughout much of the 1980s. Scholars such as William Shawcross and Sophal Ear interpret this outcome as a Cold War diplomatic compromise in which strategic considerations complicated efforts to achieve accountability, without implying endorsement of Khmer Rouge rule. Mainstream historical scholarship, including the work of Ben Kiernan published by Yale University Press, likewise rejects claims that the United States directed arms networks for the Khmer Rouge or exercised operational control over its forces. Although Cold War rivalries shaped diplomatic recognition and prolonged the conflict, the principal source of military and diplomatic support for the Khmer Rouge after 1979 remained China rather than the United States or Vietnam.

This Cold War legacy left a lasting imprint on Cambodia's post-conflict development, contributing to fragmented political legitimacy, highly centralised state authority, weakened institutional capacity and externally mediated approaches to conflict resolution. Contemporary Cambodia therefore represents a continuous historical trajectory in which rapid economic transformation driven by global integration coexists with political consolidation shaped by post-conflict state-building and the enduring legacies of the Vietnam War, Cold War intervention and regional geopolitical competition in Indochina.

30 September, 2017

16

BOSNIA'S MASS GRAVES

A HARROWING NEWS HAS COME from the Balkans in September 2017. Bosnian Missing Persons Institute has found at least 137 clusters of bones, including 86 skulls of human remains, on the cliffs of Vlasic Mountain, around the town of Travnik in Bosnia.

It is believed to be one of the biggest mass gravesites, found in Bosnia and Herzegovina, until now. These remains are possibly of the Bosnian Muslims, and Croats, who died at the hands of the Bosnian Serb Police, known as *'Red Berets,'* during the Bosnian war, in the 1990s.

Although, the perpetrators of this ethnic cleansing campaign were convicted by the country's tribunal, for lifelong imprisonment, the people associated, with the dead ones, are still seeking justice, because they have not been able to find the remains of their family members, who had just vanished, after the war.

The investigators found that the remains were found, at the bottom of the cave, and were covered, with an enormous number of rocks. This massacre at the Bosnian cliff was regarded as one of the most notorious, in its history.

The investigators of the International Commission on Missing Persons (ICMP), claim that the hidden mass graves, in Bosnia and Herzegovina would be akin to 'solving the world's greatest forensic puzzle.'

Around hundred thousand people died during the ethnic war involving Serbs, Croats, and Bosnian Muslims, which resulted, in the breakup of Yugoslavia, in 1991.

The Dayton Accords were constituted as a peace agreement, but about 2.2 million people were displaced.

During the massacre at the Vlasic Mountain, the separated men were told to hand over all their belongings and were told that they were going to be exchanged, for prisoners, at the nearby camp, but instead, they were killed, and buried, in the mountains. Only some of the men had survived, who had jumped into the river when the shooting by the Serb police had started.
The whereabouts, of most of the victims of the massacre, at the Vlasic Mountain, was unknown, until the recent investigation.

This is not the first time, an investigation of the missing persons has happened, at Vlasic Mountain. Before this, in the years 2010 and 2009, at least the remains of sixty individuals, had been exhumed, and forensic analysis had been done. Since then, the investigations have been ongoing.

Over time, the Bosnian war had been regarded as a major episode of genocide, in European history, since World War II. The cities of Bosnia and Herzegovina were regarded as abodes of cultures, but later, cities like Sarajevo and Prijedor became motifs of a war zone. The war was recorded in the first-hand narratives, of many correspondents, and sketched, in the stories of acclaimed political cartoonists, and displayed in art exhibitions.

At the end of the war, about 31,500 people were reported missing. Since then, the remains of 25,000 victims have been exhumed, from hundreds of mass graves, according to the Bosnian Institute. There are still about 6,500 unaccounted as missing people, on their registry.

Some estimates also suggest that over 40,000 people went missing in the Balkan Wars, a carnage like the Third Reich.

In 2013, the discovery of the Tomasica mass grave burial site, also made news headlines, because it was claimed that about 360 individual remains, mostly Bosnian Muslims and ethnic Croats, were found. In the Srebrenica massacre investigations, about 629 bodies were dug up.

Very recently, another mass burial site was found in the eastern town of Vlasenica. The remains were of ten Bosnian Muslims, killed in 1992.

The war also had a vivid impact on many common *Bosniaks*. Some of the relatives, of the missing members, had devoted a significant amount of time, to finding their missing ones, in the quiet woods, undermining the risks of possible landmines beneath, and occasionally encountering a human shoe, a money wallet, or a watch. However, the hope to find them has not gone away.

Each year, many Bosnian Muslims commiserate the 'International Day of The Disappeared,' on the 30th of August, by paying homage, to their dead ones, in their prayers.

The impact of the Bosnian War has left deep imprints, on our world, and it cannot be undermined, by any means. The role of the United Nations, in its peacekeeping, stooped in the following time, and the entity became unreliable, with its dysfunctional operations.

These instances of war, also called for structural reforms, because the UN has been suffering at the hands, of some superpower nations, for their vested interests, and inefficient vision. These realities have not allowed the entity to shine, in times of human adversity, in many conflict zones.

If we talk of Bosnia itself, the Dutch peacekeepers, known as 'Dutchbat,' of the UN Peacekeeping Force, still hang their heads in shame, for failing to protect an eastern Bosnian village, by being frightened, and allowing it, to be ravaged by Serb violence, in the times of war.

By just making statements, the UN has escaped from its peacekeeping action plans. It has also failed to address the dynamics of war, by helping people from many conflict zones.

Bosnia remains one of those examples, in its post-conflict period, where justice still awaits in many ways.

22 September, 2017

17

SPAIN AGAINST CATALAN REFERENDUM

CATALONIA, A NORTHEASTERN REGION OF SPAIN, wants to bid Spain, adieu. Draped in red, yellow, and blue separatist flags, many people held placards, which read' Goodbye Spain,' in the marches.

Many Catalan youths, from different backgrounds, planned for more mass mobilisation, around central Barcelona, since the first week of September 2017.

It is because they like to call themselves Catalans, rather than Spaniards. But, the government in Madrid wants to block the referendum for independence, which is scheduled on coming October 1st, 2017.

'Wikileaks' has recently published an inside story, where they accused Spanish intelligence services, and the government, of calling for moves against the referendum. Its founder, Julian Assange, strongly favours the referendum.

Reactions are coming from everywhere, in Spain. Several opposition parties, in Catalonia, like the Popular Party, and Catalan Socialist Party, have vowed not to participate, in the referendum process.

Many analysts, from the press worldwide, believe that the economic woes, since the 2008 financial crises, including chronic unemployment, have fuelled the pro-secessionism mood, in Catalonia, lately.

The region also pays more taxes, than the investments they receive, from the central government, in Madrid. This reason also has helped the cause of secession. Although, many argue that younger Catalans want to remain within Spain. This political test, if happened, might show the point of view of the majority.

Quite recently, BBC noted that Catalans marked their national day, called *'the Diada,'* with regional flag-wavering marches, and rallies in Barcelona. It reflected a massive outpour of people. Although, no episodes of usage of live ammunition, rubber bullets, or police brutality, have been recorded, until now.

However, the Spanish government is believed to have withheld several guns, that were assigned to the Catalan Police (*Mossos*), since 2016. The Spanish government, on the contrary, accuses Catalan separatist leaders, of using the national day for an independent state.

Since 2009, around three such referendums have taken place (three phases in 2009, three phases in 2010 and one phase in 2011). However, in 2014, in a Catalan self-determination referendum, an overwhelming majority of Catalans, wanted a sovereign state of their own, although the turnout had been only 40%.

The nature of these referendums was non-binding, and unofficial, according to the Spanish government, which allows the consultative referendum, on 'political decisions of special importance.'

Although, such a referendum requires the approval of both the government and the 'Congress of Deputies'

('*Cortes Generales*'). But, enactments for a secession, of any territory, are not allowed, according to Article 2 of the 1978 Constitution, which calls for national unity.

Contrarily, Arthur Mas, the former president of the Autonomy Statute (*Generalitat de Catalonia*) signed the governability agreement, on 19th December 2012, with the Catalan political party, ERC, which declared that Catalan people have genuine reasons for 'democratic legitimacy,' and 'a right to decide their future.' The Spanish government, then, had declared it a void agreement, under their Federal Constitutional Court.

Catalonia is a region, which enjoys greater autonomy, within Spain. The prosperous region, home to 7.5 million people, holds considerable powers, in education, and healthcare policy.

However, two separatist parties, in Catalonia, namely Junts Pel Si, and the CUP, led by activist Carme Forcadell, have asked its regional assembly, to suspend the speaker sessions, so that they can concentrate, on the upcoming referendum vote. The Spanish government regards this exercise, as a 'coup against democracy.'

The developments are causing stern reactions, from the Spanish government. They have ordered a criminal probe, against pro-independence Catalan mayors, who have offered municipal facilities, for the event.

Many of them do not want to be Spanish servants. The order consists of a list, of around 700 officials. It is because the supreme judiciary of the Constitutional Court, in Madrid, deems the referendum, to be an illegal act. Prime Minister Mariano Rajoy, a conservative politician, is against the referendum, as well.

The finance minister of Spain had also announced that the central government would take control of the Catalan finances. It is a move to safeguard, the regional councils, from receiving any slush funds, for the independence vote.

All bans on promotional materials, and ballot boxes, are also in effect. But these developments are not stopping people, to march for the referendum campaign. They call it an oppressing move, against the wishes of the Catalans.

In the past, 'Revolutionary Catalonia,' during and after the 1930 civil war, was largely controlled, by anarchist and socialist trade unions. It had been a stronghold of libertarian socialists.

During 1936, attacks on Spanish nationalists have been recorded, in their history, as a reaction to the withdrawal of policies, collective farming, in the countryside, and fighting against central power. It paved the way for fascist 'Francoist Spain,' in the coming years. Memoirs of George Orwell have recorded an extensive perception, of anarchist thought, in Spain.

Many Catalans, belonging to several towns and villages, have hailed these referendums, as an act of defiance, and a symbolic victory, against the central government. They view themselves as 'morally excluded,' from Spain's Constitutional Court orders, of the past.

Catalans believe, after independence, they will design a reformed tax agency, and a new welfare system, which will redefine the purpose of social security, in their lives.

In September 2017, several people attended pro-independence meetings, in places, such as Tarraco Arena, in the port town of Tarragona, south of Barcelona. An audience, of about 7,500 pro-independence activists had been recorded.

15 September, 2017

18

QATAR EMBARGO

EAST AFRICAN NATIONS ARE THE MOST recent countries, to join diplomatic protests Qatar, as the crises enter the fourth month, since June 2017. This natural gas-rich emirate, in the Gulf Region, continues to get affected, economically.

The Horn of Africa including Senegal, Chad, Niger, and Mauritania have severed ties with Qatar, many of them recalling their ambassadors. They have joined the diplomatic isolation, along with Saudi Arabia, Egypt, Kuwait, and UAE, who have restricted Qatar, from using their air space, land border, and waters.

These countries, in the Horn of Africa, have joined the gulf nations, in terms of collective solidarity. Although, Somalia has offered help to meditate, on the crises, as well.

The diplomatic consequences seem to be causing great fear, in international trade, for Qatar, which holds the third-largest proven reserves, of natural gas, in the world and is currently bidding for more infrastructural development, inside the country. The crises can spill over to pivotal construction facilities, needed for FIFA World Cup 2022.

The Qatari crisis started when the gulf coalition gave a 13-point list of demands, in June 2017, that included expelling Turkish military forces, severing ties with Iran, closing Al-Jazeera media offices, stopping payments to allegedly terrorist organisations, ending interference, in internal affairs of other sovereign countries, and being monitored for compliance.

When these demands were not met within ten days, an economic-political embargo started, and many Qatari nationals, branded as terrorist supporters, from the many Gulf States, were expelled.

Qatar has all along denied charges, of supporting radical groups, like al-Qaeda, or the Islamic State, but a report has alleged that Qatar has paid a ransom to Iraqi *Shia* militias, and Iranian security officials.

Qatar has also established military bases, in the Horn of Africa. It manages seaports there and has contributed to the region, with foreign aid, in the past.

In Sudan, the Qatari government sponsors Darfur mediation and keeps good relations. However, Saudi, or UAE military, may replace withdrawn Qatari peacekeeping forces, in Eritrea, which has previously been close to Qatar, as well, where Qatar mediated its conflict, in Djibouti, in 2010.

In the present time, Qatar will most likely lose economic competition in comparison, with other Gulf countries. Its successful national airline, Qatar Airways, has been badly affected by the blockade.

As a result, Qatar can largely no longer be a country of influence in the Horn of Africa. Factually, it is struggling domestically.

To tackle food crises, Iran and Turkey, both Qatari allies,

have sent tons of food to the crisis-ridden country, where previously 40 per cent of food came from the land border with Saudi Arabia. Qatar's stock market lost over $15 billion in these months of the embargo.

For years, the shores of East Africa have provided important logistical routes for traders to reach the Gulf region, and vice versa, mostly through Bab el-Mandeb Strait, a crucial checkpoint for oil tankers (worth 4.7 million barrels of oil and hydrocarbon products), coming from Gulf to Europe, that connects the Red Sea with the Gulf of Aden. Hence, these facts itself, indicate the importance of relations, between the Horn of Africa, and the Gulf region.

Qataris are not surprised by the crises. To counter crises, many Qatari shipping companies have shifted their regional bases, from Dubai's Jebel Ali Port, to Sohar Port, in Oman. It indicates that Qatar is making long-term preparations, for securing economic activities, such as logistic services, shipping, and passenger ferry operations. Oman may benefit from this action, from Qatari policymakers.

Qatar may suffer from economic loss, by the closure of Bab-el-Mandeb Strait. In fact, instability of any kind, from any Gulf country, would force tankers, to travel through the southern tip of Africa, instead, making logistical operations cumbersome, with higher costs, and transit time.

For a while, Bab el-Mandeb Strait has remained a lifeline, for other gulf states, like Egypt, Saudi Arabia, and Israel, and a source of a billion-dollar revenue.

These dangerous waters known as the 'Gate of Grief,' in

Arabic, have also promoted activities of smugglers and pirates, in recent times, and have also suffered, amidst the ongoing Saudi-Yemen conflict, including attacked US ships, by Houthi rebel movement. The recent debate, on the strait, due to the Qatar trade embargo, also reveals the political volatility of Gulf trade, in the area.

Quite recently, UAE also secured a foreign military base, in Bab el-Mandeb Strait, in the northern Somali region, of Somali land, which may become problematic for Qatar, if diplomatic crises continue.

It also seems, as if Saudi Arabia, and UAE, want to occupy southern Yemen, including Aden Port, Bab el Mandeb strait, and wants to isolate Qatar, which has provided aid, to build hospitals, schools, and homes, for the homeless, in many war-torn Yemeni provinces, since 2015.

'Qatar Red Crescent' has donated, over $160,000, to victims of war, in areas, that are both under Houthi control, and Yemeni government control.

Many in southern Yemen, back the 'Southern Movement,' for independence, and support UAE. The Saudis, and Yemeni government, are currently looking for any proof regarding Qataris supporting Houthis.

There also seems to be some kind of loose strategy, implemented by UAE, and Saudi Arabia, to counter Iranian expansionism, and isolate its regional allies, like Qatar, with whom it shares the world's largest gas field. It is because an Iranian-dominated shipping trade, in Bab-Al-Mandeb, including the Qatari trade, could threaten all shipping trade, through Suez Canal.

If the United States supports the current political strategy, of Saudi Arabia, and the UAE, then it will be interesting to see how the Qatar crisis will end if the Americans wish to intervene.

7 September, 2017

19

IMPORTANCE OF THE KURDISH REFERENDUM

On 25 SEPTEMBER 2017, A BINDING referendum will take place, in Iraqi Kurdistan, which was initially planned, in 2014.

This development has been criticised, by Turkey, Iraq, and Iran, as these three neighbours have always looked down upon their aspirations for freedom. They deem the referendum causing a 'greater conflict' and 'destabilisation' in the region.

A majority of five million Iraqi Kurds, voting for independence, is widely expected. Kurds always wanted a nation of their own, ever since the end of the First World War. For this cause, no one can deny that they have given the epitome of sacrifices.

When colonial powers, redrew the maps in the Middle East, the Kurdish people faced a miserable brunt, because the land they belonged to, was divided into Turkey, Iran, Syria, and Iraq.

In each of their retaliations, throughout recent history, they had been beaten, because of a stronger military opponent. Now, this is a historic time for the Kurdish people, because political progress seems to be underway.

The Kurdish referendum comes at an unfavourable time, especially, when Iraq, is amidst a civil war, propelled by

Islamic State.

The Iraqi *Shi'ite*-dominated areas are trying to oppose the upcoming referendum, but it is unclear, what political moves they have planned to prevent it.

Iraqi military organisation is dysfunctional right now, and in operational fatigue, because of their counterinsurgency missions, against the Islamic State. In the present crises, many war-torn Iraqis have increased complexities, by entering the region.

Although the last civil war happened in the mid-1990s, Kurdistan has been regarded as a major conflict zone, where notorious episodes of genocides, and ethnic cleansing, have happened, especially during the reign of Saddam Hussein's Baath Party.

In their history, the Kurdish rebellion of 1983, led to *'Al-Anfal Genocide'* (inspired by a chapter in the Qur'an). including the barbaric Halabja chemical attack by Saddam's cousin, Ali Hassan Majid, known as *'Chemical Ali,'* which resulted in the killing, of over 10,000 people, in Kurdistan. The hostilities, in the region, proceeded with Kurdish -Turkish conflict, the ongoing Iran- PJAK conflict, and the creation of a Kurdish autonomous republic in Iraq in 1991.

A referendum vote, proceeding in the coming time, would also harm the re-election prospects of current Iraqi Prime Minister Haidar al- Abadi, who is enjoying a winning success, against the Islamic State insurgency, with the help of the Iraqi State military.

In recent times, the Kurdish Army, known as *'Peshmerga,'* have been pivotal, in defeating the Islamic State, in the

'*Rojava*' territory of Kurdish Syria. Many Kurdish leaders wanted the referendum, to be held after the fall of Mosul, which eventually happened, a month back.

The White House opposes the referendum, but Israelis support it. The referendum, however, has also been criticised in some quarters, because Kurdish volunteers, and its '*Peshmerga*' fighters, who have helped thousands of Yazidi civilians escape war, in the ongoing Syrian conflict, are out of financial means. For this purpose, a $22 million aid, from US State Department has also been depleted, since last September.

The other important concern, that is rising amongst common Kurds, is the uncertain nature of the referendum. Many think that the timing of the referendum is premature, and they want their leaders, to ponder more on economic issues, of development, like paying salaried employees adequately, and diminishing their state debt, to name a few.

The expected referendum will make Iraqi Kurdistan, free of control, from the authority of *Shi'te* Arab-led government, in Baghdad. However, many common Kurds see the referendum, as a ploy against their economic mismanagement, since the last twenty-five years, with the establishment of the Kurdistan Regional Government (KRG), in 1992.

Despite this fact, figures suggest that the area has been much more developed than Iraq and other Kurdistan regions. Many nicknamed Iraqi Kurdistan, 'the next Dubai,' with annual GDP touching 12.7% between 2005-2008, and 11.8% between 2010-2012.

The region has a giant oil bed beneath, and the economy,

is oil-based, with a giant 970 km crude oil export line, starting from Ceyhan, in Turkey, to Kirkuk, in Kurdistan. The region has also attracted, around 20,000 ex-pat workers, in the past. However, the current scenario of declining oil prices has also put a great strain, on the Kurdish oil sector, and that led to declining salaries, and low purchasing power, mostly, since 2014.

Many commentators are also making fair assumptions, regarding improved economic progress, in the oil-rich region, as a largely free Kurdistan, which will not need approvals, from Baghdad anymore, for corporate investments, and foreign direct investments, in general.

There are also risks involved, with a fully initiated Kurdish independence, in Iraq. Many believe that the truest form of independence, for the Kurds, would be a united Kurdistan, constituted of all countries.

The Kurdish population in South Eastern Turkey has withdrawn their demand for independence and now wants greater autonomy. The same goes with Syrian Kurdish-controlled '*Rojava*,' which relies more on direct democratic political models, or decentralised councils.

However, the Iranian Kurds, on the other hand, are resuming their armed struggle, against the Iranian Republic.

In recent times, Iran has shelled several Iranian Kurdistan villages, largely consisting of '*Kolbars*' (Kurdish porters).

Iranian Kurdish political parties have expressed support, for the referendum in Iraq, and so have the regional Turkish Kurds.

Therefore, there is a chance that a free Kurdistan, in Iraq, in times to come, could propel a renewed cause of secession, from the Turkish Kurdistan region, when the Kurdish Workers Party have unfavourable stances amidst Turkish leaders, EU, and US lobby, and Iranian Kurdistan region, due to mid-level insurgency.

31 August, 2018

20

FARC SIGN A PEACE DEAL IN COLOMBIA

COLOMBIAN GOVERNMENT SIGNED a historic peace deal on November 24, 2016, with FARC *(Fuerzas Armadas Revolucionarias de Colombia)* rebels, the largest insurgency group that had waged a war, for over fifty-two years, in the country.

This has happened, as a revised drafted agreement, between the government, and the rebels, because of a referendum in October 2016, that was rejected by the narrowest of margins, by the people, (50.2% said no, 49.8% said yes). Many FARC-dominated areas, interestingly, had voted for the peace deal. It indicates that people, in these regions, are suffering in the war, and want a better future.

The UN Secretary-General, European Union, US Government, and the Pope, have backed the peace agreement. However, people, like former Vice President of Colombia, Francesco Santos, think otherwise. He believes that making a peace deal with rebels, holding guns, is wrong, and they should be convicted on shorter, if not longer jail terms. There are also extremist views, coming from his party, with some of his party associates believing that the 'rebels should go back to the mountains.' It is a stance, that encourages war, that the incumbent president of the country, believes as unacceptable.

War with FARC, by the Colombian government, was often regarded, as the last major conflict in the Americas. The conflict has finally been deemed to be over, as the last truckloads of decommissioned rifles, were taken out, of a remote camp, in the countryside, in northern Colombia. The rebel group handed over, as many as 8,000 weapons, and 1.3 million pieces of ammunition, after the negotiated truce.

Rebels will now transform, into a political party, although they have not announced, which individuals will lead them, in the future. They have now changed their group name to 'Revolutionary Alternative Forces of Colombia,' and aim to become a 'voice for the voiceless.' They want to represent those, who live in 'abject poverty,' and the 'honest, and good people.' These former rebels, who have turned to politics, have also announced their 2018 election alliance, with the Colombian Communist Party.

Colombia has historically suffered, from the absence of big-scale land reforms. Elites owned vast swathes of land, and common peasants suffered at the hands of the barony.

The founders of the former FARC (*Revolutionary Armed Forced of Colombia*) were small farmers, and land workers, inspired by Marxist – Leninist philosophy, and the Cuban Revolution. They had grouped, against staggering levels of inequality, at that time. It was often branded, as a rural guerrilla organisation. At their peak, about 20,000 men had picked up the gun, for the group. They also maintained their support network.

Between 1948-1958, the term *'La Violencia,'* was used for a ten-year civil war. It was largely perpetuated, by the assassination of a leading liberal politician, Jorge Eliecer Gaitan, and the return of Colombian conservatives, to power, who had seized agricultural lands of liberal-supporting peasants.

'*La Violencia*' period had led to the killing of 200,000 people, as both parties, had organised their guerrilla military units. Some leaders transformed their ideology, from liberalism to communism, later.

In the war, millions abandoned their homes, and property, media services had failed, and documented evidence of violence, had become rare.

Former FARC rebels will live in 26 demobilisation camps, where they will be involved in peace-building and development work. The former rebels also want to form a new professional soccer club. The group had also brought out more than a hundred child soldiers, according to inputs received, from the International Committee of Red Cross.

FARC rebels, who had been convicted by special courts, will avoid traditional prison sentences and will perform reparation work, such as removing landmines, from various areas.

President Juan Manuel Santos has been a winner of the 2016 Nobel Peace Prize, for his efforts, to win an end to the hostilities. The deal grants amnesty to its ex-fighters, and the group will finally enter the electoral frays, with 10 unelected seats, in the Congress, until the end of 2026.

The conflict claimed at least 250,000 lives and left around 60,000 people missing. Millions were displaced, from their homes, fleeing the bloodshed. Under the peace accord, the state presence, in remote areas, will lessen, and efforts to increase food crop cultivation will begin.

By reduction of state troops, in areas, where basic amenities like running water and electricity, are scarce, the overall conditions will likely improve, and make residents content.

As rebels will now live in transition camps, common Colombians believe that there are still inherent challenges ahead, to transform the country, into prosperity. The murder rate is very high in the country, indicating societal problems. Illegal cocaine production and the influence of drug cartels are still rampant in Colombia. There is also a debate to lessen cocoa production, in the higher realms of power, which will lead to further decreased trade of the commodity.

To act against the current truce agreement, several paramilitary groups like *Autodefensas Gaitanistas* had been distributing pamphlets, in their areas of influence, for a new declaration of war. The group had declared that the FARC peace deal was against the interests of the Colombian people.

24 August, 2017

21

KENYAN POST-ELECTION CRISES

Aﬀﬆﬂ UHURU KENYATTA FROM the jubilee party of Kenya won the 2017 General Election, on 8th August 2017, the opposition party leader, Raila Odinga, from National Super Alliance, has charged the electoral commission, of a 'computer-generated fraud,' where hackers have influenced the winning result, by logging into the account, of a senior electoral commission official.

To counter the claims, the EU delegation recently passed out a statement, about no such manipulation, at the central and local level, and has urged the people to accept the election result.

Kenya's election commission had also commented about a hacking attempt that failed, and election observers have said they saw no signs of interference, with the voting.

Analysts are also discussing, these moves, by the opposition party leaders, which seem to them, like gimmicks, to stay in the limelight, aimed to heighten chaos, in the post-election results.

Young voters have dominated the scene of Kenyan politics, over the period, constituting over fifty-one per cent of the electorate. It is a country, where eighty per cent of the population, is under the age of 35.

However, many regional political commentators, claim

that many young Kenyans have lost interest, in national politics, which may be bad for the country. The other reason can be that they did not find both candidates appealing, to lead them, and therefore want a new face to lead them.

Kenya has one of the highest unemployment rates, among East African Nations, according to a 2016 World Bank Report. One can find nearly one in five young Kenyans, without a job. Kenya is also currently suffering from a high cost of living, rising public debt, a high public wage bill, and corruption allegations among people, close to the government.

Both Kenyatta and Odinga have differed widely, on policy issues, throughout their political career. In international diplomacy, Kenya plays an important role, in the African Union Mission in Somalia (AMISOM), a major regional peacekeeping mission.

Ironically, Odinga has often called for the withdrawal of Kenya's Defence Forces (KDF), despite being the prime minister of the government that sent Kenyan soldiers to Somalia, for the first time. In contrast, Kenyatta has urged regional leaders, to deploy more troops, to counter Al Shabaab, and has called on the international community, to help with additional deployments, of military troops.

The political slogan 'Uhuru's Action Plan: More Jobs. Lower Cost of Living' might have worked for the President-elect, Uhuru Kenyatta, the second time around, despite anti-incumbency factors.

His voter base had been made up of smallholder farmers, who expected heavy investments, in agriculture, in return for their vote loyalty, as there had been a recent discontent, in the milk and coffee prices, in the country.

Kenyatta had an early advantage in the election against Raila Odinga. It is because many believed Odinga was too old, to lead the country.

This is not the first time, some sort of election crisis has happened in Kenya. If we go back in time, in the 2007-2008 election, Raila Odinga had alleged election manipulation, that time around as well, charging former President Mwai Kibaki.

Fuelling the election crises, in the 2007-2008 election, Raila had encouraged supporters, for mass protests, and as a result, police shot hundreds of protestors, including a few, in front of TV cameras, causing more violence, and controversy. That year, in Kenyan history, post-election had been regarded, as an event of targeted ethnic violence, mainly against Kikuyu people, members of former President Mwai's *Kibabii* tribe.

About six hundred thousand people were displaced, and around 1,300 were killed. Some of the people, in the community, had been locked in a church, and burned up alive, on New Year's Eve. Post-election violence also happened, during the 1992 elections, mainly in the Rift Valley province. Therefore, it seems, that the post-election crises in Kenya, are not a new thing, for the masses to endure.

In a poll conducted by Synovate, a London-based market research company, more than half of the population was unhappy, with his first election term. However, his rating improved dramatically, after 2014. A poll by Gallup, in August 2014, put his approval rating at 78%.

Raila Odinga has pleaded to fight the 'supposedly election sham,' in the Supreme Court. Odinga also used a biblical allegory, in his campaigns, positioning himself as Joshua, leading his people out of oppression, to Canaan.

Ironically, many common people are using adages against him, such as 'he is trying to weave together when he is out of thread and needles.' They also want him to retire and get isolated from politics. Several commentators believe that stable elections are not only important for Kenya but also for the rest of the African continent. Currently, the UN has urged the opposition party, to calm down its supporters.

The media also reported about several Kenyan graffiti artists, using peaceful messages, to spread harmony, in their areas. It has presumably been a reaction, against the killing of eleven people, in the post-election crises.

17 August, 2017

22

THE FALL OF MOSUL

Since the capture of mosul by the Iraqi state in July 2017, the city has been left with over five thousand destroyed buildings, including mosques, schools, and hospitals.

The bloody campaign finally ended, after nine months of intense fighting that killed thousands of Iraqis, and displaced millions of its residents.

Many observers of the war claim that there are still chances of increased suicide attacks, in the city. Many other small Iraqi cities remain under the control of the Islamic State.

However, the fall of Mosul signifies the biggest loss for the Islamic State, in terms of territorial area. But they are still inspiring people to join their ranks, which the Iraqi government calls a challenge.

Right now, the country faces big challenges in restoring electricity and rebuilding destroyed hospitals, schools, homes, and bridges, which were wrecked in the ground combat, by the airstrikes, artillery fire, and rocket attacks, carried out by the American-led coalition, to help the Iraqi troops advance. The cost of reconstruction, calculated by UN-led experts, has been around seven hundred million American dollars.

Some grand structures, including the al- Nuri Mosque, have also been pulverised in the war. Both, Islamic State, and Iraqi State have blamed each other for the destruction.

History bears witness that it was this mosque, where Abu Bakr al Baghdadi, in June 2014, self-proclaimed himself, as the Caliph of the new Islamic State, and plead to lead the Muslim community. Since 1924, the office of a caliph has not been initiated, until Baghdadi's announcement.

The motto of the Islamic State has been *'baqiyah wa tatamaddad,'* meaning 'remain and expand.'

The target maps drawn by the fighters, for the creation of the Islamic State, seem, as if, they want to bring a likeness of the Ottoman Caliphate, (the strongest Muslim empire to date), back to the current times.

They had been getting support from the regional *Sunni* tribes. Young Muslim militants have read online manuals, such as the 'Management of Savagery,' first published in 2004, a document widely popular all over the world. It describes the phases of expansionism, and campaign, a form of a chain, sweeping one country after another.

Therefore, it is not hard to believe that Islamic State has been strongly backed by Islamic theology and discourse, with time, to make Muslims return to their original way of scriptures, and in making militant reforms.

Islamic State fighters have governed the area with the strictest forms of Islamic law, which include beheadings, and holding women as sex slaves. American war commanders claim, that the intense fighting in Iraqi cities, against the Islamic State, has reminded them of the years of World War II.

New York Times journalists, who reported from Mosul,

with the help of their fixers, witnessed Iraqi soldiers 'trading volleys' with Islamic State snipers, from the roofs of nearby buildings, in the city.

Mosul has been a war spot, not in the recent past, but since the US-led invasion in 2003. It is regarded as a bastion of Iraq's *Sunni* Muslim minority and maintained the tradition of supporting Saddam Hussain and his Arab Baath Party.

Shadow administration of the Islamic State, during the early days of their control, had forced many Iraqi military officers into exile, and many were assassinated. Some had even joined ISIS.

General Abdul Wahab Al Saadi, who leads the Iraqi Counter Terrorism Service, described the recent perching of the Iraqi flag, on the banks of Tigris, as a symbolic victory against the Islamic State.

Currently, several thousand people are in the process of returning to places like western Mosul. According to UN data, about 676,000 people have left Mosul. These events indicate that the war has turned Iraqis into war refugees.

Earlier in May 2017, Iraqi Prime Minister, Haidar al Abadi, declared eastern Mosul liberated from Islamic State fighters. The Iraqi parliament had also recently passed a law, for the initiation of Iranian-backed *Shia* militia fighters into the state force, who were known as Popular Mobilisation Forces.

Islamic State militants have used C4 in their bombs, in Iraq, during the war. The most surprising thing that the Iraqi forces found lately, was the usage of a weapon-making factory, in a church, including plastic sachets of white explosive powder.

Foreign nurses, working in the war, have witnessed civilians coming to hospitals, with crushed torsos and limbs, besides, nursing Iraqi forces, who came injured with bullet wounds, during their combat campaigns.

One of the many reasons for the formation of the Islamic State in Iraq had been the division between *Shi'ite* and *Sunni* communities, the political disparities that had turned rife from time to time, in the country, and the Arab world in general.

The divisions had recently sparked off during the *Shi'ite*-led government of former Prime Minister, Nuuri Kamal al Maliki. Many viewed his rule as a project drawn against *Sunnis*, and to frighten them.

People following an extremist religious ideology, due to the presence of ethnic tensions, are not holding the country together.

Hence, for these religious divisions, many *Sunnis* viewed the presence of the Islamic State, in Iraq, as a protection against their abuses.

This sectarianism, had, inspired many young boys to pick up the gun, and they went to war joining Islamic State ranks.

The fall of Mosul indicates a sudden transformation in the region.

9 August, 2017

23

PERSECUTION OF ROHINGYA MUSLIMS

IT HAS BEEN AROUND ONE YEAR SINCE 2016 when Aung San Suu Kyi-led National League for Democracy (NLD) has been posted with power.

Widely regarded as a champion of human rights, and a celebrated political prisoner, she has now come under the scanner for her cold shoulder, to a UN fact-finding mission, to investigate the ongoing human rights abuses, by security forces, in the Rakhine state, against the Rohingya Muslim minorities.

Aung Sang Suu Kyi denied visas to members of an investigative mission, endorsed by the UN Human Rights Council, earlier in 2017. Many think that it will be very hard, even for Suu Kyi, to reverse this decision, in a country, where military power occupies a crucial role.

The military still controls important quarters of the national assembly, including budget formations, resistance to constitutional changes, and clearing ordinances, without the approval of the cabinet.

The leader had been under house arrest for fifteen years, during the military rule. Therefore, the influence of democratic institutions and accountability commissions, in the country, is still largely unknown today.

As many as ninety thousand Rohingya Muslims have fled their villages, since the last fall in October.

In response to the killing of nine police officers, at a border post, by a Rohingya militant group, the military instituted a massive crackdown in the area, that lead to hundreds of arrests.

In joint operations, police and military have allegedly burned down homes, raped and abused women, and killed hundreds of Rohingyas. These events also largely indicate the press freedom in the country, because the overall media reaction related to it, has been low.

The World Food Programme estimates that more than eighty thousand Rohingya children may need treatment for malnutrition, in the area, a figure that reflects worsening humanitarian conditions, following the recent surge of violence.

Quite recently, the American government and Human Rights Watch, an international advocacy group, decried Myanmar's refusal to grant visas, and have asked the country to cooperate with the United Nations.

To refute international outcries, the Myanmar government believes that the presence of a UN fact-finding mission will heighten political tensions and that they are doing their investigations. It seems that the UN mission is losing its influence, in the country.

Quite lately, the government opened Rakhine to a group of foreign journalists, with government escorts, but unfettered access is still denied, throughout the Rakhine area.

Rohingya Muslims are largely forgotten and continue to get mistreated. Access to healthcare and education is denied. They are even restricted to travel to a neighbouring village.

Since 1994, they have not been allowed to get birth certificates from the government, and require government permission to marry. The Rohingyas are also denied citizenship, along with Tibetan people, Anglo-Burmese, Burmese Gurkha and Burmese Pakistanis, in the country.

Rohingyas are perhaps one of the most mistreated communities in Burma, along with the Karen community, whose villages, religious buildings, and schools have also been burned, and their people killed and displaced (about fifty thousand Karen refugees now live in deprived shantytowns at Mae La camp, Tak in Thailand).

In 1978, the military tried to expel the Rohingya population into Bangladesh through mass arrests, destruction of mosques, and villages and confiscation of lands. These measures eventually ousted a quarter of a million Rohingyas into Bangladesh, in six months. In 1990, the country again began displacing the Rohingya population into 'strategic villages,' near military bases and started settling the local Buddhists.

The Rohingyas are under assault from all sections of society. The country has followed a strategy of 'Four Cuts,' which has denied the population land, food, shelter and security.' This eventually led two hundred fifty thousand Rohingyas across the Naf River, into Bangladesh, during the 1990s.

In 1992, when a new border security called *Na Sa Ka* was formed, Rohingyas were subjected to slave labour, for Buddhist settlers, on Rohingya land, for construction purposes. Therefore, the ethnic prejudice against the community in Myanmar is historical, and not recent.

In 2011, the Bangladeshi government blocked about thirty-three million, in UN humanitarian aid, for the Rohingya refugees. Only twenty-eight thousand refugees were recognised and kept in two camps in the Cox's Bazar, a fishing port town, south of Chittagong. Over time, over two hundred thousand refugees were dispersed throughout the hills of Cox's Bazar, where they struggled to survive on their own, and were constantly in danger of disease, violence, and starvation.

Muslims are believed to have settled in Burma, since the fifteenth century. They have lived when the Burmese leaders have followed a largely Buddhist policy, or 'Burmanisation.' Some historians and scholars are of an opinion that Rohingyas are indigenous to the Rakhine state, originally part of the independent kingdom of Arakan that was annexed in 1785, by the Burmese kingdom.

While on the other hand, the government narrative maintains that most of them are illegal immigrants, of South Asian origin, who migrated during Burmese independence in 1948, and Bangladesh Liberation War, in 1971.

In an internal audit reviewing the UN conduct in Myanmar, which had been sent to the UN secretary-general, the organisation in the country was tainted as 'glaringly dysfunctional'.

The reviewers compared the functions of the organisation with notoriously mismanaged crises in Sri Lanka, during the civil war.

A recent Guardian article commented that the UN office in Myanmar has failed to have 'senior level engagements,' and has largely been treated like 'a non-entity.'

2 August, 2017

24

CREATION OF MALOROSSIYA IN UKRAINE

RUSSIAN-BACKED REBELS WHO HAVE BEEN fighting in eastern Ukraine, have proclaimed a new state, for the areas, they control, which are around nineteen provinces in July 2017.

The rebels have named it '*Malorossiya*' or 'Little Russia,' a lingual derivative of a historical ethnic province, completely coincidental, to the current day, where once its ruling feudal baron pled allegiance to the *Czar*.

The history of conflict goes back more than thirty-three years. Around ten thousand people have been killed, and 1.6 million people have been displaced.

Since 2014, Moscow has consistently denied involvement in the fighting in the area. This claim has been contested though. Some even claim that Kremlin has for a long time backed an insurgency and that many rebels have been Russian soldiers.

The Associated Press members have documented how Moscow has been propping up the separatists, in Ukraine, with funds, weapons, and recruits.

The ongoing insurgency had resulted, from the Euromaidan Movement, which led to the resignation of Ukrainian President, Viktor Yanukovych.

Civil unrest had escalated in his time, because of a decision, where the government chose to suspend an association agreement, with the EU, and instead, chose to stay close with the Euro-Asian Economic Movement, and Russia. These events ultimately lead to the 2014 Ukrainian Revolution, followed by the War in Donbas, Russian military intervention, and the annexation of Crimea by Russia.

Many view this new state, comprising of self-proclaimed Donetsk, and Luhansk Republics, as part of a modern-day expansionist Russia.

It was the rebel leader, Alexander Zakharchenko, from the Donetsk side, who declared his area, as part of the Federation of Malorossiya. He has even declared a three-year state of emergency and has also decreed their flag, as a variant of that flown by Bohdan Khmelnytsky, the famous Cossack leader, who led a revolt against Poland-Lithuania, in the mid-17th century.

A new constitution will also be drafted under broad discussions. These declarations provide some clues, about the existing ideas, and political approaches, of some groups in the region.

Alexander Zakharchenko led the Minsk Protocols negotiation, for the War in Donbas peace process, in 2014. He also represented the self-proclaimed Donetsk People's Republic, in 2015, agreeing to the Minsk II peace treaty, to alleviate the ongoing war. It has now been decided that the capital of the area will remain Donetsk, with Kyiv as a centre of 'historical-cultural importance'.

Historically, the term *'Malorossiya,'* meaning 'Little Russia,' has been used synonymously with *'Novorossiya,'* meaning 'New Russia.'

Tsarist administrators called the area *'Cossack Hetmanate,'* what is now modern-day Ukraine. It was once part of the Tsardom of Moscow, and of a 'triune Russian nation' (an all-powerful Russian empire, consisting of Great Russian, White Russian, and Little Russian subjects, living in smaller nation-states), inspired by the Russophile ideology.

Patriotic Ukrainians, however, regard the name *Malorossiya* as offensive, and synonymous with Russian imperialism.

Minsk Protocols did reduce fighting, to some extent, but many minor skirmishes continued. When rebels launched offensives in Ukrainian-controlled areas, it resulted in a direct violation of the Minsk Protocols.

Under the deal, the rebels had to return control of the territories they had captured to Kyiv, while Kyiv had to allow a local election there and grant wider autonomy to the region. Many leaders had regarded these protocols as the 'last chance,' for the resolution of the conflict. But, nothing of sorts has happened.

The other measures of the observed unconditional ceasefire had also failed, including the release of war prisoners, and constitutional reform. Over time, Ukrainian leaders had vowed to fight against the rebels, till the 'liberation of Ukrainian lands from Russian occupants,' while rebels vowed to fight till victory.

Several opinion makers believed that it had been too dangerous for the Ukrainian air force, to fly in the rebel-controlled areas lately, as the rebels have brought down about twenty planes.

Russians call their military presence in the area through the prism of 'humanitarian convoys' that had come without the permission of the Ukrainian government.

In 2016, Russian President Vladimir Putin justified the incursion, as 'defending the Russian-speaking population in the Donbas.'

It will be important to note, that the region of Crimea, is in a state of a 'frozen conflict,' because Russia militarily controls the region, while Ukraine still claims it, as their part.

As of now, the rebels will continue their control of all-important southern and eastern provinces.

The White House, under the leadership of Donald Trump, has been thinking of arming Ukrainian armed forces, as a way of defending further inclusions, in the country. Although, Kremlin has warned to act against any such military moves.

If a conventional war happens, the Ukrainian military would likely have a hard time making Russians retreat in the war.

However, if one goes by the polls, the most recent that happened in May 2017, conducted by The Centre for East European and International Studies, called as ZOiS Report, most respondents in the contested eastern territories were in favour of remaining with part of Ukraine, and one-third supported a special status, for the territories, within Ukraine.

Thus, the recent declaration of a new state led by Alexander Zakharchenko, by no means, reflects the overall preference of the local population.

The political leadership is also not united. It has also turned out that the leadership of Luhansk did not know about the creation of the Malorossiya federation in Donetsk, and therefore they chose to refute reports of their participation.

Will both self-proclaimed rebel territories (DNR and LNR) get stitched in the future? Probably, time can only tell.

26 July, 2017

25

ONGOING BALOCHISTAN CONFLICT

BALOCHISTAN HAS BEEN NOTORIOUSLY nicknamed as 'Pakistan's Killing Field.'

After four insurgencies in 1948, 1953, 1978 and 2004 (which continue to this date), it has largely been a known fact that political and socio-cultural alienation is a pressing issue in the largest province of Pakistan.

When Pervez Musharraf, former president of Pakistan, launched military offensives inside tribal administered areas, including Balochistan, the strategy had been quite inconsistent, unlike the strategy of Muhammad Ali Jinnah, the founder of Pakistan, who made cordial political relations with *Balochi* leaders, like Nawab Akbar Bugti, in events, like the grand ceremony of Sibi Durbar.

Jinnah had visited Balochistan, and made pacts with *Balochis*, in his last years of life. Also, he had made some inevitable promises, including their decision to join Pakistan, through a referendum, and safeguarding their interests, by ensuring autonomy, and direct supervision of the Governor General's office.

The times and perceptions have changed now. Musharraf, in his self-imposed exile, in London, called *Balochis* 'terrorists' in 2012. Since then, military offensives are believed to have made the collapse of law and order, in a province, which was believed to be the 'steel frame' of the country.

Suicide bombings, attacks on trains, and buses, unidentified killings, and disappearances have been rife, in the area. The growing presence of the Islamic State will further complicate the insurgency landscape. Violence by targeted killings has continued unabated.

Balochistan is the largest province of Pakistan, although sparsely populated. Many a time, *Balochis* have been treated with contempt over government policy matters, because Pakistanis believe their agitation, is insignificant because they make up only 3.6% of the total Pakistani population.

The Balochis believe that their oppression has demographic factors to it as well, including a huge influx of 1.5 million Afghan refugees, in their land, during the Afghan war, of 1979.

For the development of Gwadar port, many jobs and plots of land have been given to outsiders that have heightened resentments. They believe the Government of Pakistan to be nothing, but 'Punjabi Fascism'.

Over a period, the central government has also been at odds, over their exploitation of Sui gas fields, located in the Bugti Agency.

Gas was discovered in Balochistan in 1953. The locals have been alleging that they have not been getting a fair share of the deal, for their resources. They also believe that the construction of highways, during Musharraf's time, was an intention to bring more troops, into the province.

When Pakistani troops were sent on orders of martial law, in 1958, the leader of the Khan of Kalat was arrested. He, along with his sons, was then executed. Historically, the

Marri Balochis, have continued to rebel, since the 1960s. In 1973, at the time of Z.A. Bhutto's government, many of their villages were destroyed. At the end of 1977, over ten thousand Balochs had been killed. These facts of history, serve as harsh reminders, of humiliation, and betrayals.

Historically, Balochistan covered the southern part of *Sistan o Balochistan* Province in Iran, in the west, the Pakistani province of Balochistan in the east, and in the northwest, Afghanistan's Helmand Province. It is even before the devolution of British India, the land of the Balochs remained divided.

The stern neglect of political rights had given rise to local militancy over the years. Baluchistan Liberation Army formed in 1999 has remained active between 2005 and 2006, in subversive activities in Marri-Bugti areas, attacking gas installations, military and para-military forces, and civilians including *Hazara* minorities. Balochistan Republican Army has also made a shift, from political struggle to militancy.

Balochistan has also remained one of the poorest regions. Fifty-eight per cent of their land is uncultivable, due to water scarcity, and sixty-two per cent of people do not have access to safe drinking water. Many *Balochis* also seem to be unhappy with CPEC on political grounds.

When Akbar Bugti was killed in a military operation, in 2006, in the Bhamboor mountain range of Kohlu, he was quickly declared their national martyr. He was depicted as a lion, in the local folklore. Hours after his death, over five hundred people were detained in riots throughout the province, with many of the Baloch protesters targeting Punjabi-owned properties and businesses in Quetta, worsening already volatile ethnic divisions across Pakistan.

The movement for autonomy, which he had also supported at one point in time, had quickly changed into a movement of independence. It had changed because Bugti was believed to be the only link with Pakistan, and after his killing, a secessionist movement emerged.

Bugti leaders had put one billion rupees and one thousand acres plot of land, as a bounty, on Musharraf's head.

Since then, a policy of catch and kill followed, and too many bodies appeared, mysteriously in villages. Messages such as *'Pakistan Zindabad'* and *'Long Live Pakistan'* were engraved on their dead chests.

Many Baloch scholars and journalists were targeted, and it signified a decapitation of their cultural and social values.

In March 2016, when Pakistan claimed that a spy named Kulbhushan Yadav was tasked by India's RAW, to carry out extremism in Pakistan, to bomb a hotel in Gwadar, it stirred new controversies.

Conversely, Pakistani nationalists also cite a Gallup-DFID UK poll, stating that only a minority population around thirty-seven per-cent, support independence in Balochistan, and hail the steps for democratisation.

19 July, 2017

26

RESOLUTION OF CYPRUS FAILED AGAIN

IT SEEMED THAT THE CYPRIOT LEADERS would finally break the ice, for a settlement. In a series of negotiations from June 28th to July 7th in 2017, Nicos Anastasiades, Cyprus's president, and Mustafa Akinci, his Turkish-Cypriot counterpart, were determined to reunite the divided island, but the deal, unexpectedly, turned into a failure.

In the Swiss town of Crans Montana, the prospect, of broking a deal, for the resolution of the Cyprus dispute was high. An enthusiastic debate on dinner, at the Swiss Alpine Resort, stretched throughout the night.

The deal eventually turned into a failure, because the arduous talks, on power-sharing arrangements, reshaping territorial boundaries, and several economic agendas, of the Cypriot state, were declared unsuccessful.

Many fear that it could have been the last chance, for the country, for a successful political resolution. Before this, in 2004, there had been a chance for a political solution, when Cyprus entered the European Union.

President of Cyprus, Nicos Anastasiades, had called for the total withdrawal of Turkish troops. But, after the failed talks, altering the presence of troops, remains a distant dream.

Leaders of both sides (Turkish, and Greek sides of Cyprus)

met under UN mediation, with the foreign ministers of Greece, Turkey, and Britain (the colonial superpower governed the island, from 1878 to 1960, and still retains military bases there). A European Union representative was also an observer.

In terms of duration, many compare the Cyprus dispute, with the Israeli- Palestinian dispute. In the past, the UN security council, in numerous resolutions, has set the framework of a Cyprus solution, which must be 'bi-zonal,' with a separate parliament, and a 'bi-communal federation,' with equal political rights, for the two Cypriot communities.

Geographically, it is the Greek Cypriots that occupy the larger area, in the south. UN monitors a buffer zone, between the two communities, which is called the Green Line. This line separates the north of the country, from the south. Some ten thousand people live in several villages and work on farms, located within this demilitarised buffer zone. The village of Pyla is famous for being the only village, in the zone, where original Greek and Turkish Cypriots live, side by side.

In current times, there seems to be less recognition of Northern Cyprus, internationally. Many political analysts believe that the presence of Turkish troops, roughly thirty thousand, who cover thirty-seven per cent of the northern island, is a human rights violation. The observers them as 'occupiers,' in an EU member country.

This presence of troops also gives outside powers, such as Turkey, a political advantage. The country, even self-declared the area, as the Republic of Northern Cyprus, but Turkey cannot annex it, at present times.

In the past, the Cyprus dispute was mainly seen as a dispute between the people of Cyprus, and the British colonial empire, for self-determination. The British had annexed the island from the Ottoman Empire. But, as times changed, the dispute was mainly seen as an ethnic dispute, between Greeks, and Turks, living on the island.

The history of the island reflects a blood feud. Historically, the Turkish invasion of Cyprus, in 1974, had happened, soon after the successful military coup, by the Cyprus National Guards, aided by a Greek military junta, to install a Greek irredentist nationalist regime, in the country. It was a plot to annex the island, as part of the Republic of Greece.

In the year of 1964, Cyprus and Turkey also engaged in confrontation, during the Battle of Tillyria, as civil warfare, between the ethnic Greek, and Turkish Cypriots. Hence, it seems, that the historical relevance, of the resolution, carries significance. Cypriot Turks, living on the island, have been seen, as a repressed minority, mainly since the 1960s.

Yearning for peace, a communal gathering had happened lately, in the heart of the capital, of Nicosia, on the crossing point, between the Greek, and Turkish sectors, by eighty-five parties. It consisted of trade unions, and civil society groups, of both communities. They had demanded, from the community leaders, an agreement, according to the wishes of the people.

Before the failed agreement, the activists had even signed a declaration, stating that the common vision of Greek and Turkish Cypriots, is the only deal that is legitimate, and will lead to reunification, and peaceful coexistence in Cyprus. Hence, it seems, that many Cypriots still seem to be optimistic about a solution, even after forty-three years of separation, since 1973. But, their aspirations, unfortunately, have been repeatedly falling upon deaf ears.

There are different perceptions too. If one goes by the general perception, of many individuals, inside the country, the people of the Greek Cypriot side are against the separation of their country. However, young Cypriots, who were born after the partition, are not interested, in reunification, anymore.

The leaders, who come from the Greek Cypriot side, want Turkey to step down, as a guarantor, for the solution. They rather want European Union to be the guarantor of security, in their country, as they are of the political opinion that the security of one group cannot be overlooked, at the cost of another group's security.

12 July, 2017

27

TORIES MANAGE AN ALLIANCE

The UK general election of 2017 produced one of the most precarious political settlements in recent British history. Theresa May's Conservatives won the largest number of seats (317 out of 650), but fell short of an outright majority, leading to a hung parliament. In the aftermath, the government entered a confidence-and-supply agreement with Northern Ireland's Democratic Unionist Party (DUP), led by Arlene Foster. The DUP's 10 MPs became decisive for maintaining Conservative governance.

The election had been dominated by Brexit. May called a snap election on 18 April 2017, hoping to strengthen her parliamentary position ahead of negotiations with the European Union. However, the gamble weakened her authority instead. As reported by BBC News and The Guardian, the campaign was marked by her decision to avoid live televised leader debates, instead relying on controlled interviews and set-piece appearances. The political backdrop remained the 2016 referendum, after which Prime Minister David Cameron resigned and the UK voted to leave the European Union, despite significant opposition in Scotland and Northern Ireland.

The DUP agreement, concluded on 26 June 2017, provided support to the Conservatives on key votes including the Queen's Speech, budgets, and Brexit-related legislation. In return, the government committed additional funding for Northern Ireland, including up to £1 billion in extra spending across areas such as infrastructure, health, and education. As the Financial Times and BBC News reported, this sparked controversy, with critics arguing the deal gave Northern Ireland preferential treatment compared with other UK regions, particularly economically deprived areas in England. Labour politicians and others described it as politically motivated and unfair, raising concerns about the UK government's traditional claim of neutrality in Northern Irish affairs under the Good Friday Agreement.

Public and political reaction was immediate and polarised. Protests took place in Westminster, and petitions opposing the arrangement gathered significant signatures. Critics warned that reliance on the DUP—whose socially conservative positions differed sharply from mainstream UK parties—risked complicating Brexit negotiations and domestic policymaking. Commentators in The Guardian and The Independent highlighted concerns that the deal could intensify regional and constitutional tensions, especially given that Northern Ireland had voted to remain in the EU.

At the same time, the European Union maintained pressure for a structured timetable to conclude withdrawal negotiations. In practice, the key deadline became October 2018 for agreeing a withdrawal treaty text, allowing time for ratification before the UK's planned departure date in March 2019. Within Britain, Theresa May's government faced continued instability, as even a small number of Conservative rebellions could threaten its survival in Parliament. Meanwhile, the Labour Party under Jeremy Corbyn gained momentum, positioning itself as an alternative to austerity policies and Conservative Brexit management.

Domestically, the wider context included ongoing austerity pressures, strained public services, and uncertainty over the rights of EU nationals. The UK government later introduced the EU Settlement Scheme (from 2018 onward) to regularise residency status for EU citizens living in Britain, including those with long-term residence rights.

In retrospect, the DUP agreement symbolised the fragility of May's government. It ensured short-term survival but deepened perceptions of political instability and dependence on small-party leverage. The arrangement became a defining feature of the post-2017 political landscape, illustrating how Brexit had transformed parliamentary arithmetic into a source of chronic volatility.

For Labour, the episode reinforced its argument that the Conservative government lacked a stable mandate, while for May, it marked the beginning of a prolonged struggle to maintain authority in an increasingly fractured Parliament.

4 July, 2017

28

RETURN OF GULBUDDIN HEKMATYAR

GULBUDDIN HEKMATYAR RETURNED TO Afghanistan, in April 2017, after an exile of twenty years.

Mysteriously underground, and presumably hiding, in the rugged mountainous terrain of Pakistan, his return marked countless prior negotiations, on his role, in civil life, his rights, and his privileges.

He had been nicknamed 'the butcher of Kabul,' after killing thousands of people, between 1992 to 1996, with rockets and artillery, in the civil war. He also served as Afghanistan's prime minister, an office he held, for a brief period.

With a sense of political opportunism, he now vows reconciliation, with the Taliban, through dialogue.

At least two hundred people welcomed him, in the eastern Laghman province of Afghanistan, where he had been conducting meetings, with his former party members, lately. Common Afghans had mixed feelings about his return, as posters of him, and his party were seen torn, on the streets.

Hekmatyar, a former anti-Soviet commander, in the 1980s, has called Taliban renegades, his 'brothers,' and calls them to join the 'caravan of peace'.

With an ageing face, white beard, and traditional black

turban, he appeared in public rallies recently, after striking a twenty-five-point deal, with the Afghan President, Ashraf Ghani, in September 2016. This peace accord marked his return, to his country, in April 2017.

Supporters of Hekmatyar believe, that his actions, in the 1990s were taken in self-defence. His political party, Hezb e Islami, is known for deadly attacks, on US forces, since their invasion in 2001.

Interestingly, now his name has been removed from the UN list of active terrorists. He was also designated as a terrorist, by the US states department, in 2003. These developments have given rise to new controversies. After all, what makes politicians and pivotal organisations endorse a former warlord, for mediation, in Afghan politics? It remains unclear.

The Soviet-backed, socialist People's Democratic Party of Afghanistan, fell into a civil war, between 1989 to 1992. After that, intense violent years were witnessed, in Afghanistan, till 1997.

The Taliban had ousted Hekmatyar's faction, and other factions, after their triumph in Kabul, during that time. The developments paved the way for Taliban rule. At this time, it was believed that Hekmatyar first sought refuge in Iran, right after the war.

His ideology is inspired by the Muslim Brotherhood, and Maududi's Jamaat-e-Islami.

Calling the Islamic war against Western forces as 'unholy,' 'in vain' and 'illogical,' in his speech, in April 2017, he at the same time, endorses the doctrine of jihad, and has anti-Western sentiments. This has made it difficult to categorise Hekmatyar's political rationale.

At a time, when the Taliban has criticised his return, his role as a collaborator, can become reactionary. Maybe, his return will implicate further divisions, in Afghan politics.

Ashraf Ghani seems to be playing a dangerous game, in an attempt, to mend the broken political, and social fabric, for democracy, and respect for human rights, and fundamental freedoms, in Afghan society.

How can a peace deal with a ruthless warlord by a civilian government ever make moral sense? His faction of guerrilla fighters received the bulk of arms, and money funnelled in by the CIA to defeat the Soviets because he was seen as ruthless, and close to the Pakistani government, and ISI, an individual, tailor-made for the American proxy war.

On the contrary, Ashraf Ghani sees Hekmatyar's return, as a first step toward taming the insurgency that has been ravaging Afghanistan, for more than a decade.

The deal also called for the release of prisoners, from his former militia. This is at a time when Ghani has lost public support when the Afghan economy is struggling, and security concerns are rising. Civil war survivors and human rights groups have condemned his return.

Hekmatyar's return also proves a major setback for regional leaders, like Ahmad Zia Masoud, and Ata Mohammad Noor, both representing Jamiat-e Islami, the major Tajik political party. This could propel them for an ethnic cause, for the next presidential election, in 2019. It is because Hekmatyar has made it open to make an alliance with Hezb-e-Islami Afghanistan (HIA), to form the country's largest political faction that could result as a deciding factor, in the 2019 elections.

Pashtun nationalist parties, like Afghan Millat Party, will also support Hekmatyar, in the next election, in a country, polarised politically, on ethnicity. The resentment of Hekmatyar against the Hazaras is widely known among the public. Also, Uzbek leaders like Abdul Rashid Dostum, who helped Ashraf Ghani achieve a wide vote base, in the last election, have recently accused the president, of breaking the promises, on government appointments, for his party.

For this breach, his political exile to Turkey sanctioned by Ghani, could make it easier for Hekmatyar, to achieve major strides, in the next election.

Council for Protection and Stability in Afghanistan, a coalition of jihadi parties, many of them close to Hamid Karzai, would also be more than happy to endorse Hekmatyar against Ashraf Ghani's shaky National Unity Government, which has failed in addressing various constitutional issues, and in initiating reforms, by succumbing to domestic political pressures.

In other words, the next Afghan election will not be for the common Afghans, it would rather be Pashtuns fighting against Hazaras, Uzbeks and Tajiks to attain power. In this grim political scenario, Hekmatyar could have a major role to play.

26 April, 2017

29

PROTESTS ON THE STREETS OF BRASILIA

BRAZIL HAS BEEN WITNESSING UPHEAVELS since 2015. Around thirty-five thousand people marched in the capital and other cities in May 2017.

Angry demonstrators have set fire to several ministerial buildings in Brasilia. Commuter buses have been burned. Slogans of Communist sickle and hammers have been sprayed on the walls. This graffitis called for 'Death to the Bourgeois.'

To quell upcoming protests, there has been a heavy police presence on the streets. Rubber bullets have been fired.

There also has been an investigation surrounding the usage of live ammunition, on protestors.

Now, people are demanding the resignation of President Temer, fresh elections, and economic plans, set by the current regime, to be withdrawn.

Unions of key sectors, political parties, and activists, stand as one people, to bring a change, in their country. General strikes have been called. Proposals to bring changes to labour laws, and the pension system, have angered the common man.

Temer had proposed a minimum age, for retirement, which would compel many employees, to work longer, receive a pension, and reduce payouts, in a country, where many workers retire with full benefits, in their 50s.

Recent polls suggest that over ninety-two per cent of people want new elections, and there is less than a ten per cent of approval rating, for President Temer.

These events indicate the unhappiness citizens have developed, against their current leader. As the result, the stocks and their currency are plummeting. One minister has also resigned.

There have been two kinds of protestors on the streets of Brazil lately, especially since the impeachment of Dilma Rousseff, in 2016.

The first types of protestors were the working class, largely anarchist, with no favoured politician.

The second types of protestors were defenders of Dilma Rousseff, who were paid, made of a mix of pro-government thugs, and special interest groups, defending their government propaganda.

The first group defended the investigations and more economic freedom, and the second defended the parties and politicians.

Rightly after the new election, President Michel Temer has come under investigation, by the Supreme Court, for giving an alleged bribe, to silence a former jailed party ally. The protests in Brazil have not put the president on second thoughts. He wishes to stay in power, and lead the country.

In a wiretapped conversation, Temer discussed bribes. He appeared to tell Joesley Batista - one of the owners of Brazil meatpacking giant JBS - to maintain payments to Eduardo Cunha, the vilified, and imprisoned former speaker, of the House of Representatives, in return for his silence.

Former presidential candidate, Aecio Neves, and the former finance minister, Guido Mantega is also said to have been involved, among the eighty-three alleged ministers.

Eduardo Cunha, formally of Temer's Brazilian Democratic Party (PMDB), led the impeachment against ex-president Dilma Rouseff that made Temer take the realms of presidential power. However, Eduardo was sentenced to fifteen years, in prison, for corruption, in March. Temer had been the vice president, in her government.

In *Petrobas* scandal called 'Operation Car Wash' dozens of politicians, and executives, have been convicted, for bribery, and embezzlement charges. The executives of state-controlled oil company *Petrobras* allegedly accepted bribes, in return, for awarding contracts, to construction firms, at inflated prices.

Brazilian construction conglomerate, *Odebrecht*, which suborned government officials, around the world, for years, has also been exposed by investigators. The company had an entire unit that served as a bribery department.

All these developments have made the common man furious because the elites have been robbing their country blind.

The 2015-16 mass protests, in Brazil, that eventually led to the impeachment of Dilma Rousseff, were due to these same reasons of blatant corruption. Dilma Rousseff, in the past, had tried to block the Petrobas investigations.

Luiz Inacio Lula da Silva, Rousseff's predecessor, who was regarded as a leftist icon, in Brazilian politics, was also accused of money laundering, and misrepresentation, including a scandal surrounding a beachfront home, that he had not disclosed he owned, and had made costly additions to it.

Since Temer became president, people have also been unhappy, with his stances, on the environment, and human rights, as well.

Temer himself has written two proposals, to reduce the protection of six hundred thousand hectares of forest, in the state of Pará, which is an area equal to Jamaica. This is at a time when deforestation has risen to twenty-eight per cent.

Also, the indigenous people have land conflicts with the farmers and ranchers. When three thousand indigenous people marched the streets of Brasilia, some time back, they were met with police brutality.

Brazilian politics has been synonymous with corruption, for decades, as politicians never seemed to have been held accountable, for their actions.

Currently, Brazilian politics is sending shockwaves, to the world, with its corruption probes. Many think that Temer should step down.

These scandals are also threatening vulnerable leaders, from Panama to Peru, in Latin America.

15 June, 2017

30

ROUHANI'S SECOND TERM

AFTER ROUHANI WON HIS SECOND Presidential term in Iran, in May 2017, hard-line conservatives have once targeted him. His rivals have accused him of winning on voter fraud.

After taking 58.6 per cent of the forty million votes, core political issues, in Iran, are once again back, in the limelight.

The elections have come at a time when the neighbouring Arab region is in turmoil.

Rouhani had mostly targeted the middle-class vote, in his campaign, and that had resulted to be the right strategy for him.

His election also proves a setback for Iran's Revolutionary Guards, who control vast industrial zones in Iran. They had banked their support on his controversial conservative rival, Ebrahim Raisi, involved in the death of thirty thousand political prisoners, in the 1988 Iranian massacre.

Rouhani had won because of collective anger, in large cities, particularly because of urbanites, for anti-Rouhani stance, on state-run televised, and radio programmes.

During the last four years, Rouhani was also in continuous discord with the judiciary, largely influenced by the conservatives, and directly controlled by the supreme leader.

His critics believe that the 2015 landmark nuclear deal that ended sanctions, by his regime was a failure, and divided Iran. They did not want him to reach the Western world. Rouhani also has been accused of being a foreign pawn, for corruption, and for espionage, to list a few.

Thousands of common Iranians face water shortages, pollution problems, unemployment, and inflation, in present times. In places like Shahriar, a town in Tehran, homeless people beg for food all day, and sleep in graveyards, in pre-prepared graves. It has shocked common Iranians and reflects the poverty looming in the country's capital.

Rouhani must make a progressive economic plan to address these problems, at a time when his economic management has come into question. Promises for a fifteen billion American dollar investment, and three to five billion American dollars for the poor and the needy, have come forward.

Iran is OPEC's number three oil producer. Rouhani plans to sign deals with oil majors like Russia's 'Lukoil' and France's 'Total,' very soon. Development of oil fields, and increasing production capacity, are also on his agenda, which would increase oil sales, and improve the economic sectors.

During his election campaign, he also talked about the removal of remaining sanctions and boosting tourism. To add to that, his supporters also believe that talking about human rights strengthened his voter base.

The Iranian Green Movement, which started in 2009

collapsed slowly, as their demands for the cancellation of Ahmadinejad's second term were not met, but it gave Iran a successor in Rouhani, who had years of accumulated political, and economic failures, in front of him.

Rouhani must fix a deal for other problems as well. He must mediate on competing for foreign policy views, with the guardian council, which overviews the democratic institutions in Iran. Till now, he has also been unsuccessful in getting his reformist comrades, out of house arrests.

Also, Saudi Arabia has been a hostile country, supported by western powers. They have been deploring the nuclear deal. As the result, Americans supporting *Sunni* Movement, in the Arab region, have been slowly isolating Iran, in many regional matters.

When shared Saudi-Israeli intelligence has reached an unprecedented high, during the Trump administration, it will be difficult for Iran to change its regional stance, on Hezbollah, in Lebanon and the Syrian civil war. On the contrary, Rouhani, in the past, had been busy negotiating frozen assets, for Iranian military disbursals, in places like Bahrain, the Horn of Africa, and elsewhere.

Trump administration had also expressed its interest, in talks with Iran, in the recent past. It will be interesting to see how dealings with the Trump administration will shape up, when Americans believe that Iran supports regional instability, and sectarian divide, in the region. Many analysts believe that the resolution of the Syrian civil war, through diplomacy, may ameliorate Iranian - Arab relations, but its realisation seems out of sight, right now.

Recently, there has been an outpour of debate, on media

machines, relating to whether it is right to brand Rouhani, as a moderate. Executions and tortures have happened, in Iranian prisons, right after the election.

Many analysts say that he is allowing IRGC (Iran Revolutionary Guard Corps) and *Quds Force* to expand their interests, in places like Syria, Iraq, and Yemen. He had also been part of the 1979 revolution that called for public executions.

In his tenure, about three thousand Iranians have been already sent to the gallows. Many view his military and intelligence background as controversial, and implicate him, as a suppressor of Iranian civil liberties.

As a secretary of SNSC (Supreme National Security Council), in the past, he was responsible for closing several newspapers, and satellite dishes, and quelling the protests.

In the streets of Tehran, several graffiti describe Rouhani as a 'demagogue' and 'king of executions.' These occurrences, in the country, have put his political leanings into question.

7 June, 2017

31

POLITICAL REACTIONS IN POLAND

POLAND HAS SUDDENLY BECOME volatile, because its citizens believe that their freedoms are at risk.

In December 2016, thousands of Poles marched the streets of Warsaw, to register their protests, against constitutional amendments. People have chanted slogans like 'Free European Poland!' and 'Poland is here!' Some had lips sealed with tape, to suggest freedom of speech was threatened.

Supporters of Civic Platform Party (PO), and Committee for the Defence of Democracy, a social organisation, had called for a 'Freedom March,' in which protestors carried Polish, and EU flags, aiming to show the resentment, that Poles, in general, have developed against the ruling Law and Justice Party (*PiS*), and their authoritarian leaders.

They fear that the attitude of the current government would oust them from the European Union, and NATO membership, for their lack of respect, for political rights, and democracy.

The estimate of attendance had been about ninety thousand. In May 2016, the protests the government reached a figure of two hundred forty thousand. A pro-Euro parade, called the 'Schumann Parade,' also took place, in Warsaw, lately.

The major cause of unrest has been changes made to the

Constitutional Tribunal, Poland's highest court, where a two-thirds majority out of fifteen judges, could make it difficult for laws, to get invalidated.

However, government officials have regarded these events as a propagandist evasion, and insist that the rights of people are ought to be respected. On the contrary, the European Commission has announced an investigation into this enactment and has said that these changes threaten the rule of law.

The ruling government was also unhappy over the European Commission's decision of appointing former prime minister, and Civic Platform leader, Donald Tusk, as its president, because they believe members of political groups should not be made heads of the European Commission. Therefore, the protests in Poland, have resulted in international political implications.

PiS leader, Jaroslaw Kaczynski holds a considerable say, in party matters. He calls for European Commission powers to be reduced, including regulation of state aid of industry, to national control.

Kaczyński also has had some success in reviving the Visegrad Four Group, of central European countries (V4)— Poland, Hungary, the Czech Republic, and Slovakia, as a vehicle, to currently rebuff Belgium, and Germany, in some policy matters.

His main reason for opposing Donald Tusk's reappointment to European Council, as president, is that they view him as a foreign pawn, and the other reason is the mysterious plane crash tragedy, in western Russia, that killed Polish President, Lech Kaczynski, in 2010.

Jaroslaw has accused Russian President, Vladimir Putin, and Donald Tusk, serving in prime ministerial office, at that time, of the tragedy, and not the bad flying conditions, that resulted in the crash. He still vows to bring justice, for the mysterious death, of his twin brother.

The ruling party, PiS, played the wild card of immigration influx, during the campaigns, and swept the election, after a decade. Now as they rule, its leaders have come under fire, for controlling state-run enterprises, and curbing media freedoms, of Polish TV, by sacking the directors and installing government loyalists. Most of the programmes, functioning now, are government propaganda programmes that safeguard party interests.

These developments are indicating the political rhetoric, on which the current government is functioning, and defending its stances. The opposition party, PO Liberals, seem ahead in the opinion polls, right now.

After the fall of Communism, Poland had been regarded as a vibrant Eastern European country. Its history was filled with multiculturalism. But, since the advent of the organised Jewish holocaust, by Nazis, in places like Auschwitz, Treblinka, Sobibor, Belzec, and other places, mono-culturalism is a belief, shared by many far-right Poles, in the country, today.

Many still share the historic cultural belief, about Jewish immigrants, being foreign, or hostile. Even now, many far right-wing Poles rout for a united Christian, democratic Poland, and symbolise all types of immigrants with contempt. They believe immigrants try to impose foreign values, and bring certain infectious diseases, into the country.

In November 2016, when *PiS* party won the election, dozens of people had gathered, near the city hall in Wroclaw, burning an effigy of a Hasidic Jew, to protest the adoption of refugees in Poland.

They had also been of an opinion that Islamic refugees are not war refugees, but rather economic refugees, and 'terrorists.'

Hate crime is also on a rise in Poland, where once its culture was regarded as its splendour. One can witness graffitis of blue *swastika* emblems, glorifying Nazism, on the streets of Poland.

In Gdansk, a Jewish cemetery was desecrated in 2016, and its streets are filled with racist banners, carried by the youth featuring Klu Klux Klan, and Nazi General characters.

These occurrences highly indicate the growing tension and lack of tolerance in Poland. The country remains divided now, and it is a cause of concern, for the region.

4 June, 2017

32

VENEZUELA IN PUBLIC CHAOS

THE STREETS OF VENEZUELA ARE LIKE a battlefield. The blue smoke of teargas engulfs Caracas, the country's capital. Thousands of people have been marching on the streets, to end the rule of Nicolas Maduro's socialist government beginning March, 2017.

People have been joining protests, from the slums of Petare to low-income quarters of Caracas city, such as El Valle, and La Vega. Graffiti such as *'Abajo La Dictadura,'* meaning *'Down with Dictatorship,'* in Spanish, greet the photojournalists on the streets.

It was on this 207th anniversary of Venezuela's independence, from Spain, when over two million people protested the workings of the government. The event had been called the 'mother of all marches,' by the international media.

The critics of Nicolas Maduro, think, that his, rewriting the constitution, will be a final blow to their democracy. While many of his supporters, belonging to the United Socialist Party, known as *'Chavistas,'* have marched the streets, holding his figurine, and the constitution book, in their hands, several opposition leaders think that Maduro is instigating the violence, and shielding his dictatorship, by discrediting the mass movement.

Nicolas Maduro believes that there is an economic war going on, propelled by domestic and foreign enemies. He thinks that his right-wing opponents are elitists, on the pay roll of a US-backed plot that wants to overthrow him, and his socialist government.

His opponents, however, shun him as a tyrant, because they believe that he does not want to initiate a new election, neither wants to give more autonomy, to the legislation, and neither wants to release hundreds of activists, in jails.

After the death of Hugo Chavez, Nicolas Maduro defeated Henrique Capriles, in an election, by a narrow margin. The present situation shows that the nation is divided on political issues.
Maduro has called for a dialogue, but the opposition has rejected all forms of discussions. On the contrary, a referendum to impeach the president has been blocked, some time back.

Several political analysts, based in Venezuela, believe that five hundred forty legislative members, elected by Maduro, cannot decide for millions of common masses, which, in a way, is a violation of the basic tenets of democracy. They also accuse the Venezuelan Supreme Court, of being filled with Maduro's loyalists, some with dubious qualifications. People loyal to Maduro, have been controlling state administration.

Looking at the current scenario in Venezuela, the economy had started to disintegrate, at the time of the second re-election of Hugo Chavez, the deceased leader, once loved by his people. Since then, oil prices have also declined, dramatically. Inflation stands at a whopping seven hundred forty-one cent, in 2017, causing enormous human suffering.

At a time, when young men, with hoods and masks, burn

cars, throw Molotov cocktails, at police, spraying gasoline, and set people ablaze, the government cannot afford to send more military reimbursements.

One of Latin America's wealthiest countries, the economic situation of Venezuela is on the brink of a recession. People have been starving, hospitals are not functioning well, amidst brutal state control. Children lie on the floor of the hospitals. Medicine is also running short. People wait in long queues, in supermarkets, to buy commodities, like milk, and sugar.

There is no electricity, in many parts of the country, and a multitude of people live on the streets. Opposition supporters have been banging empty pots, and pans, from their home windows, to show their resentment.

Several women groups have also joined anti-Maduro protests, holding white roses in their hands. It also included old men and women in wheel chairs, but they have met with police brutality.

In several streets of Caracas, masked protestors called *guarimbas* have been stopping running cars, for forced payments, by making street barricades.

About three hundred forty-six businesses have been ransacked. Pro-government motorcycle gangs called *colectivos,* and security forces have used heightened aggression, against the protestors. Armoured vehicles have run over protestors, on the streets.

As a result, about fifty-five people have been killed, and over a thousand injured. About two thousand seven hundred have been arrested. The graveness of the situation, indicates, that Venezuela is slipping into dangerous chaos, making the situation out of control.

Analysts believe that violence occurs in response to police crackdowns, on protestors, thus making a vicious cycle of barbarity.

In Chavez's hometown, in the western city of Barinas, his childhood home has been set ablaze. Demonstrators have also razed at least five of his statues, to the ground. Businesses have been shut, and roads have been barricaded, in Barinas, which was once regarded, as the cradle of Chavez's Bolivarian Revolution.

29 May, 2017

33

IMPACT OF PANAMA PAPERS
INVESTIGATION

IT HAS BEEN JUST ONE YEAR since April 2016, when Panama Papers were leaked to the public. Some 11.5 million digital records exposed the dark deeds of the corporates running away from tax evasion, international sanctions, kleptocracy and from fraud.

Panama Papers (also known as Mossack Fonseca papers) burst the scene by shaking governments and triggering scores of investigations around the world. Even now, the papers are giving rise to new controversies.

The impact of the Panama Papers has been widespread, with investigations launched in 80 countries, questioning political leaders, business oligarchs, sports personalities, and others. About 400 journalists collaborated and analysed the leaks.

It is, perhaps, the biggest data, journalists have worked with. This leak has been bigger than the US diplomatic cables, released in 2010, and the secret documents given to Edward Snowden, in 2013.

An anonymous whistle-blower, John Doe, leaked documents, from the Panamanian Law Firm, Mossack Fonseca, to a German reporter, Bastian Obermayer, working for the newspaper, Suddeutsche Zeitung. His motives for exposing the papers were financial corruption, and income inequality, around the world.

After that, the Washington DC-based International Consortium of Investigative Journalists (ICIJ) published the full document on their website, for which they were awarded a Pulitzer Prize, in explanatory reporting.

Perhaps, the biggest achievement of these papers is that it has put attention to shell corporations, and tax haven countries, including Panama itself, which had a notorious reputation, for many decades, in this matter.

Tax haven practices, in Panama, started in 1919, when American oil giant companies used to register their ships, in Panama, to escape US taxes, and regulations.

According to a Norwegian research journal, Wall Street helped Panama introduce tax-free laws, to let entrepreneurs start doing business, in Panama. Since then, the country passed strong laws, dealing with corporate, and financial secrecy.

These laws attracted many mafia groups, dictators, and greedy businessmen, to hide their stolen loot. Ever since the rise of international financial activities, in the recent past, usage of tax havens, and contentions against it, have dominated the financial press, and the debate surrounding it. The case of the Panama papers can be cited as a major example.

The law firm, the accused, has maintained that they have been victims of a computer hack and that their company data has been misinterpreted.

However, the scandal has exposed billions of offshore dollars, being flown into property markets, soaring up real estate market prices, in places such as London, for example.

The papers also exposed dealings of wealthy celebrities, corruption of businessmen, and personalities, in sports, and its governing bodies, like FIFA.

The documents reveal that 143 politicians, and their close associates, around the world, used tax havens.

Among the national leaders with offshore wealth are Russian President, Vladimir Putin, Pakistan Prime Minister, Nawaz Sharif, Ayyad Allawi, Vice President of Iraq, Petro Poroshenko, president of Ukraine, Alaa Mubarak, son of Egypt's former president, and Prime Minister of Iceland, Sigmundur Davio Gunnlaugsson. The Maltese prime minister has also been summoned on the issue.

According to several leading economists, tax havens do not give any positives to a global economy. They believe that the curse lies in the money flow. Trillions of illicit dollars flow out of these countries. The outflow is much more than the foreign aid, these client tax havens receive, to develop their economies.

The economists further believe, that countries, that are tax havens, suddenly become liable for outside people, and detrimental to people, who live there. This whole process, thereby, undermines domestic institutions, and social cohesion.

As a result, the domestic government becomes suddenly liable to international elites. We can relate these economic realities to tax havens, in our world today.

The scandal also prompted the European Commission to set up an enquiry group comprising 65 members. The law firm had its offices closed in several countries, and it had to fire many employees. At one point in time, the Panamanian media reported that the firm was down to only forty employees, from six hundred people a year before. Its owners were arrested, and their accounts had been frozen.

Mossack Fonseca had acted as a registered agent for more than 200,000 companies. The accused Panamanese law firm acted on instructions from third-party intermediaries, usually accountants, lawyers, banks, and trust companies. These facilitators were mostly concentrated in Switzerland, Luxembourg, the United Kingdom, Hong Kong, and UAE.

A recent poll, done by Reuters, shows that the level of transparency, regarding shareholders, and directors, has not improved, a year after the Panama Papers leak, when a general perception, of a tax clean up, by the wealthy, was expected.

21 May, 2017

34

MACRON GETS FRANCE

EMMANUEL MACRON'S VICTORY OVER Marine Le Pen in the 2017 French presidential election marked a decisive break with France's post-war political tradition. By defeating the far-right candidate in the second round and succeeding François Hollande, Macron not only disrupted the immediate rise of the far right but also dismantled the dominance of France's traditional governing parties. Sworn in at the Élysée Palace at the age of 39, he became the youngest French head of state since the establishment of the Fifth Republic— an emblem of generational change and political experimentation. Contemporary international press coverage highlighted the symbolism of his youth, with outlets such as BBC News, Reuters, and TIME noting the historic nature of his ascent and its implications for both the European Union and post-Brexit politics.

Macron's campaign slogan, "Ensemble, La France," resonated with an electorate weary of ideological stagnation and economic pessimism. Yet the election outcome revealed as much about systemic collapse as it did about popular enthusiasm. The Socialist Party's near implosion reflected a broader crisis of social democracy across Europe, while the National Front's defeat demonstrated its continued difficulty in translating protest politics into governing legitimacy. Macron rose to power not because voters embraced a coherent centrist project, but because many rallied defensively to block extremist alternatives. Contemporary commentary in major

French newspapers, including *Le Monde* and *Libération*, frequently interpreted his victory as evidence of the collapse of traditional party structures and widespread voter disillusionment with established political formations.

A former investment banker and protégé of François Hollande, Macron's rise was unconventional. He had served briefly as economy minister in the outgoing Socialist government but had never previously contested elected office before launching his presidential bid. His decision to run as an independent centrist—outside both the Socialist Party and the traditional centre-right—was a calculated gamble that capitalised on widespread voter disenchantment with partisan politics. Yet his outsider image sat uneasily alongside his elite professional background, raising questions about whether his politics could genuinely transcend France's entrenched socio-economic divides. Contemporary analysis in the Financial Times noted that Macron's technocratic style reassured financial markets while simultaneously fuelling perceptions among some voters that his project represented continuity with France's governing elite.

Macron's ambition to reshape parliamentary politics by inducting members of civil society and enforcing gender parity signalled a commitment to institutional renewal. This aspiration faced an immediate test in the 2017 legislative elections, where securing a parliamentary majority became a key measure of his authority. While institutional rejuvenation was promised, critics argued that political novelty alone could not substitute for ideological coherence or durable grassroots organisation.

Reporting in Politico Europe noted that Macron's parliamentary slate combined large numbers of political newcomers with experienced administrators and policy professionals, reflecting both institutional renewal and organisational inexperience.

Economically, Macron inherited a France characterised by strong labour protections and persistent unemployment. His pledge to reform labour laws—particularly through executive decrees *(ordonnances)* designed to accelerate policy implementation—was framed as modernisation but provoked concerns about executive overreach. Trade unions, long central to French political life, feared an erosion of hard-won protections under the guise of flexibility. His €50 billion investment programme, inspired in part by Nordic-style economic planning, prioritised ecological transition, vocational training, public services, and innovation. However, this agenda was complicated by parallel commitments to reduce public spending, lower corporate taxes, and shrink fiscal deficits—objectives that often pulled in different directions. Contemporary reporting in The Guardian observed that Macron's labour-market reforms were broadly welcomed by employers' organisations and business groups, while trade unions expressed concern about the potential weakening of worker protections.

Macron's broader challenges were substantial: reducing unemployment, improving economic growth, managing fiscal constraints, strengthening internal security amid persistent terrorist threats, and sustaining France's military engagement in the Sahel, particularly in Mali. These pressures exposed a central tension in his presidency between economic liberalisation and social protection, and between state authority and market reform.

On the European front, Macron's election was widely interpreted as a temporary reprieve for the European Union during a period of political strain. Brexit, economic stagnation, rising Euroscepticism, and the administration of Donald Trump had weakened the bloc. Macron positioned himself as a vocal defender of European integration, warning that without substantive reform, populist pressures would intensify. He advocated a range of federalising proposals, including a eurozone budget, a eurozone finance minister, joint debt instruments, and the completion of the banking union. While these proposals addressed structural weaknesses in EU governance, they encountered significant reservations in Germany, particularly regarding deeper fiscal integration and debt-sharing mechanisms. This Franco-German divergence underscored enduring asymmetries at the heart of the European project. Macron's ability to advance reform thus depended heavily on France's domestic economic performance and its credibility within EU power structures.

On immigration, Macron rejected border closures while emphasising integration through language acquisition and civic assimilation. At a time of increasingly restrictive migration politics across Europe, France under Macron maintained a comparatively liberal and humanitarian discourse. He expressed concern for asylum seekers and marginalised migrant communities while simultaneously supporting stronger administrative enforcement mechanisms, reflecting a balancing of humanitarian and security considerations.

In foreign policy, Macron signalled both continuity and assertiveness. France maintained its longstanding policy of supporting Israel's security while also endorsing a negotiated two-state solution and Palestinian statehood. This included continued engagement with organisations such as the *Conseil Représentatif des Institutions juives de France (CRIF)*, although domestic political controversies occasionally emerged around related issues. His relationship with the United States and Russia was more openly confrontational. Macron publicly challenged Donald Trump on NATO burden-sharing, climate policy, trade protectionism, and immigration rhetoric, while also supporting EU sanctions against Russia following the annexation of Crimea and reaffirming the Minsk framework. Early disagreements with the Trump administration over climate policy, multilateralism, trade, and NATO were widely covered by international media as emblematic of Macron's increasingly assertive diplomatic style.

Domestically, Macron introduced a series of institutional reforms aimed at restoring public trust. These included restrictions on hiring family members by elected officials, partial reduction in the size of parliament, enhanced transparency requirements, and limits on the eligibility of candidates with certain criminal convictions. His advocacy of digital governance and streamlined legislative procedures reflected a technocratic approach to institutional renewal. Critics, however, warned that efficiency-driven reforms risked weakening deliberative democratic practices rather than strengthening them.

Ultimately, Macron's presidency embodied both opportunity and paradox. He sought to unify a fragmented political system while simultaneously representing the elite structures that many voters had rejected. Whether his reforms would genuinely democratise French politics—or merely reconfigure managerial centrism in a new institutional form—remained an open question. His success depended not only on policy innovation but on his ability to reconcile reform with inclusion, authority with accountability, and economic modernisation with social consent.

Macron's victory in 2017 was therefore both a moment of rupture and a source of uncertainty. It temporarily contained the rise of the far right, dismantled the dominance of traditional political parties, and reconfigured the structure of French politics. Yet it also exposed the fragility of centrist politics, the contradictions embedded in reformist agendas, and the enduring scepticism toward elite-driven political renewal. His presidency remains a test of whether liberal-centrist governance can sustain both legitimacy and effectiveness in an era of political fragmentation.

16 May, 2017

35

TURMOIL IN MACEDONIA

Political theatrics appeared in the Macedonian senate in April 2017, when people wearing balaclavas and draped in a yellow and red flag, of their country, exchanged punches, with another group of men, dressed in shirts.

Scenes had translated from war of words to fighting. These rebels were supporters of the Macedonian Conservative party, who were protesting the appointment of its first ethnic Albanian parliamentary speaker, Talaat Xhaferi.

Macedonian 2016 protests, also known as *'colourful revolution'* have inflated the crises, in 2017. In 2016, European countries, such as Italy, Serbia, Germany, Bulgaria, and Croatia, called for peace.

The ongoing protests have triggered new ethnic tensions and constitutional crises. Hundreds of protesters, some of them armed, and masked people had stormed the senate building, and attacked representatives, displaying an unprecedented form of anarchy. Police, in retaliation, had thrown stun grenades, to disperse angry crowds. Journalists, too, have been hospitalised.

The Macedonian political system has been in disarray, for the last two years. Elections gave no party a clear mandate, to form the government.

Since December 2016, Macedonia is without a genuine functioning government. However, the Social Democrats managed to ally with ethnic Albanian political parties, by agreeing to their demands, for granting them certain concessions. But several demonstrators, on the streets, deem this alliance as unholy. The Macedonian interior minister has already offered his resignation, and President Gjorge Ivanov has called for emergency talks.

It was sixteen years ago, when minority rights of Albanian rebels brought Macedonia, to the brink of civil war. Western diplomacy was believed to have ended it.

Once part of Yugoslavia, it gained independence in 1991. The region lies in the hotbed of ethnic tensions, war, and even genocide.

The country also has several political, essentially linguistic, disputes, with Greece. Most recent is where Macedonians are accused of stealing their country's name from a Greek province, just south of the Macedonian-Greek border. Both countries have many aspects of Hellenistic culture in common. It was due to this reason, that Greece blocked Macedonia, from joining NATO, and the EU. Hence, Macedonia is trapped in uncertain diplomacy, and cannot be deemed, a stable country, right now.

In 2015, an agreement called 'Przino Agreement,' drafted by four leading Macedonian political parties, allowed an early election, last December. However, the previous government had been involved in a wiretapping scandal that included communications of 20,000 ordinary citizens, for several years, including its ministers, in the cabinet. These facts have infuriated the public. The tapes revealed widespread corruption, misuse of power, and security mishaps.

Macedonia is currently ranked 111 out of 180, by the

2017 Press Freedom Index. It has also seen a rise in political prisoners. There are problems of poverty and unemployment. Mundane clashes often happen between political parties.

Many analysts believe that Nikola Gruevski, who served as prime minister, from 2006 to 2016, still controls many quarters of police power, and intelligence agencies, and has been responsible, for the ongoing parliament protests. His party still controls almost half the votes in the assembly, but he has not been able to form the government.

New controversies are also emerging. Leading American - Hungarian investor and philanthropist, George Soros, has been accused of sponsoring 61 organisations, to fuel unrest, in Macedonia, with $9.5 million funding, through his initiative Open Society Macedonia, to overthrow the government.

About 2000 protestors are demanding new elections, outside EU headquarters, in Skopje. These events, in the Balkan country, indicate that elections have worsened the political crises, instead of ending a two-year-old turmoil. It is because the protestors feel that Albanian political parties are trying to instil a form of minority supremacy.

Protests are still going on, because many Macedonians feel that their sovereignty is under threat, particularly when Albanian minority leaders want the Albanian language, as another official language, in the Balkan country.

International mediation is underway. Several high-ranking US officials have arrived to end the political tension. They view the appointment of the Albanian speaker as legitimate and want to discuss reforms, needed for Macedonia's Euro –Atlantic integration. It demonstrates that Americans are opposing the concerns of the protestors.

The protests, in Macedonia, are also simmering tensions in Serbia, and the neighbouring countries, where troops have been deployed, on country borders, amidst rising fears.

Russia, on the other hand, has been blaming the Americans, for their stances, of going against the will of the protestors. These events, do indicate, that both powers want their presence in the region.

It is still unclear how things will progress, in the coming time, when most of the Macedonian public, wants an end, to the current assembly sessions.

8 May, 2017

36

NORTH KOREA IS REACTING

UNITED STATES IS WILLING TO ACT both with military combat, and political diplomacy, with North Korea under the current global scenario.

President Trump is paranoid about stockpiles of nuclear weapons, which North Korea possesses, and wants their immediate removal. It is because Kim Jong-Un has increased missile testing, since he took over the country, in 2011. That is why, a military strike has already been discussed, in the White House.

Americans think that North Korea is not a regional problem anymore, but an international problem. Fox News poll cites North Korea as a bigger threat to the United States, than ISIS, and believes, that it is the US military, that can stop North Korea's nuclear program, and diplomacy will not yield any productive measures.

The United States has already sent a nuclear-armoured submarine to the region, to boost its military strength. It is working for harsher sanctions against the communist country. Japan, also, has entered a military alliance, with the US, and has sent its warships, to join the drills.

Americans have had a history of hate relationships, with major communist countries, of the world. Under a mutual defence treaty signed with South Korea in 1953, about 28,000 US troops were already deployed, near the region, and warplanes rotate the sky, on regular deployments.

In 1994, North Korea and the US agreed to a framework, where North Korea was to freeze its nuclear development capabilities, in return for economic concessions. In 2005, both countries agreed to respect each other's sovereignty and promised to exist peacefully, to normalise relations. But the times have changed.

North Koreans have dodged imposed UN sanctions, since their first nuclear test, until now. With the help of foreign investments, they are progressing with their nuclear programme.

In this serious situation, to seek defensive measures, the United States has installed THAAD (Terminal High Altitude Area Defence) anti-ballistic missile system, at South Korean sites, which North Koreans, Russians, and Chinese, believe, is a serious security threat, in the region. ASEAN nations are also expressing grave concern, over the recent developments.

United States has also piled up the pressure, in the recently convened UN Security Council meeting. They are also requesting foreign governments, closer to diplomatic missions in Pyongyang, to work on decommissioning North Korean nukes.

United States leaders are accusing China, of doing nothing, on the issue, although, China wants an end to North Korea's nuclear programme. Chinese leaders claim that they have worked very hard, to bring both parties to the table. Russia, too, wants a constructive dialogue, between the two countries.

China, which is an ally of both countries, and involved in political tension, can act as a pacifier, but a highly complex situation has evolved.

Many intelligence agencies, contrarily, accuse Chinese politicians are acting like mute spectators, on issues, where Chinese truck companies are assisting the North Korean states, for launching missiles. Also, some Chinese companies have been accused of helping North Korea, extract radioactive substances, necessary for the development of nuclear weapons. Therefore, new controversies are emerging.

Pyongyang is spending highly on military research and development. A lot of military hardware has been boosted on military parades, which make missile launches, from ground launchers and submarines, harder to detect. Testing and missile development have increased twenty-fold, highly indicating the aggressive stances of the North Korean regime.

James Martin Centre for Non-Proliferation Studies cites that four Korean missiles have been already successfully tested, capable to fly up to 3500 kilometres (some estimates suggest up to 4000 kilometres). Other two other missiles are in development that can reach up to 11,500 kilometres (possibly into the mainland United States). The tested weapons can carry conventional, biological, and chemical warheads and are likely capable of reaching the west coast area, of the United States.

North Korea prefers to be in retaliation. Although a tiny peninsula in area, it boosts one of the world's largest militaries, a hard-core communist approach, and fervent nationalism. It has recently been releasing massive missile exercises, probably 300 to 400 artillery drills, on its state media. The country warns of an all-out war with the United States and does not fear its military advances.

Many geologists believe that underground nuclear tests, near one of the world's deadliest volcanoes, Mount Paektu could premature its eruption, in northern North Korea, near the Chinese border. Its 20-kilometer molten magna could affect the world's climate, with its plumes of deadly sulphur, especially in China, when winds enter the country, during the eruption.

Conversely, United States, having the most advanced defence systems, in the world, has always dictated, and likes subordinate powers, to protect its national and foreign interests, for many decades. This stance is not going well with North Korea.

It seems that Trump does not mind having a nuclear war, with North Korea, but prefers talks right now. The military consequences in haste, however, can become catastrophic.

1 May, 2017

37

AFTERMATHS OF ARAB SPRING

OPPRESSION OFTEN BECOMES A CHANNEL through which revolutions emerge. When uprisings erupted across the Arab world in 2010 and 2011, they were driven by demands for dignity, political freedom, and social justice, and they spread rapidly across several countries as long-standing frustrations with authoritarian governance, corruption, and economic stagnation came to the surface. Jack Shenker, reporting for The Guardian from Cairo during the early stages of the Egyptian uprising, described the Arab Spring not as a sudden explosion but as the culmination of years of accumulated anger against political repression and worsening socio-economic conditions. The New York Times, in its contemporaneous reporting from Tunisia and Egypt, similarly pointed to structural problems such as high unemployment, inequality, and weak economic management, while Al Jazeera's coverage emphasised how digital communication platforms accelerated mobilisation by amplifying voices that had long been excluded from official public discourse.

Among the countries swept into this wave, Tunisia is most often described as the closest case of political transition toward democracy. After the fall of Zine El Abidine Ben Ali in January 2011, Tunisia moved toward a new constitutional order, culminating in the adoption of a constitution in 2014 and the holding of competitive elections that same year. Even so, reports by the International Crisis Group have consistently noted that Tunisia's transition remained fragile, constrained by persistent economic challenges and institutional weaknesses that limited long-term consolidation. In other parts of the region, the trajectories diverged sharply. Egypt, Libya, Syria, Yemen, Bahrain, Morocco, and Algeria each followed distinct paths marked by varying combinations of reform, repression, and conflict. Patrick Cockburn, writing in The Independent, observed that the uprisings unleashed political forces that existing regimes struggled to control, while fragmented opposition movements often failed to develop unified leadership structures capable of sustaining revolutionary momentum. The Economist, in its early analysis of the Arab Spring, similarly argued that while the protests exposed deep structural grievances, they rarely translated into durable institutional transformation.

Nowhere were these contradictions more evident than in Egypt. Mohamed Morsi's presidency, which began in 2012 after Egypt's first competitive presidential election, quickly became politically polarising amid escalating economic pressures and deepening institutional conflict. The Financial Times reported that his government struggled to establish authority over a divided state and an increasingly assertive military establishment. Following mass protests in July 2013, Morsi was removed from power by the armed forces, an intervention that marked a decisive turning point in Egypt's post-revolutionary trajectory. The subsequent crackdown on dissent reached its most violent expression in August 2013, when security forces dispersed sit-ins at Rabaa al-Adawiya and al-Nahda squares in Cairo. Human Rights Watch, in its detailed investigation All According to Plan, documented that the dispersal resulted in at least 817 deaths and described it as one of the largest killings of demonstrators in recent history. The Washington Post's reporting at the time also described the extensive use of armoured vehicles and live ammunition during the operation. After Abdel Fattah el-Sisi assumed the presidency in 2014, political space contracted further, and Reuters reporting on subsequent legal proceedings noted that Morsi received multiple prison sentences in cases involving charges such as incitement and alleged espionage, reflecting a broader return to centralised state control.

As political order fractured in parts of the region, non-state armed groups gained strength in several contexts. In Egypt's Sinai Peninsula, Wilayat Sinai, an affiliate of the Islamic State, carried out a series of attacks, including the downing of Metrojet Flight 9268 in 2015, which killed all 224 people on board and was later attributed by multiple investigations to the group. At the same time, domestic political tensions persisted, including protests in 2016 against the transfer of the Tiran and Sanafir islands to Saudi Arabia, which Reuters reported were met with arrests and security crackdowns. These developments reflected a broader pattern in which political dissent continued to surface even as state authority became more centralised and restrictive.

In Bahrain, the response to unrest was swift and heavily securitised. The authorities moved quickly to suppress protests that emerged in 2011, particularly those rooted in Shia communities calling for political reform. Human Rights Watch documented widespread arrests, prosecutions of activists, and allegations of torture during detention, while also noting that the government framed the unrest as influenced by external actors, particularly Iran. This narrative was frequently used to justify a broad security response that significantly reduced political space and limited opposition activity.

Algeria followed a different trajectory, characterised not by a singular revolutionary rupture but by recurring cycles of protest. Even before the Arab Spring, the country experienced frequent demonstrations over housing shortages, unemployment, and inflation. Throughout the 2010s, Reuters and other international reporting consistently described ongoing protests across various regions and sectors, reflecting persistent socio-economic grievances. Despite this sustained unrest, Algeria's political system remained largely intact, shaped in part by the legacy of the civil conflict of the 1990s, which continued to influence public caution toward systemic upheaval. Protest, in this context, functioned more as a recurring form of social pressure than as a direct pathway to regime change.

Morocco's response combined controlled reform with institutional continuity under the monarchy. Constitutional reforms introduced in 2011 expanded certain parliamentary powers, but ultimate authority remained firmly with the king. Economic pressures, including periodic droughts affecting agricultural production, continued to strain rural livelihoods. At the same time, the unresolved Western Sahara conflict remained a central geopolitical issue. United Nations estimates have long indicated that tens of thousands of Sahrawi refugees continue to live in camps near Tindouf in Algeria, displaced since the conflict escalated in the mid-1970s. The Moroccan-built defensive structure known as the Berm, stretching roughly 2,700 kilometres, has been documented in United Nations monitoring reports as part of the ongoing territorial division. Analysts writing in Le Monde have repeatedly described Western Sahara as a persistent fault line in North African politics, shaping diplomatic relations and limiting regional integration.

In Syria, peaceful protests that began in 2011 escalated into a prolonged and multifaceted civil war involving the Assad government, opposition groups, extremist organisations, and external powers. United Nations human rights investigations documented widespread violations committed by multiple parties, including extrajudicial killings, siege warfare, and forced displacement. Several chemical weapons incidents were investigated by international bodies, including the Organisation for the Prohibition of Chemical Weapons, which attributed multiple attacks to Syrian government forces, while other cases remained disputed or inconclusive due to contested evidence and access limitations. The conflict produced massive population displacement, widespread urban destruction, and one of the largest refugee crises in modern history, as documented by the United Nations High Commissioner for Refugees.

In Yemen, the uprising initially led to a negotiated political transition under a Gulf Cooperation Council framework, but this process collapsed as armed conflict escalated following the Houthi takeover of Sana'a in 2014 and the Saudi-led intervention in 2015. Financial Times reporting has emphasised that the war is shaped by both internal political fragmentation and wider regional rivalries, particularly between Saudi Arabia and Iran. The United Nations has repeatedly described Yemen as one of the world's most severe humanitarian crises, with widespread food insecurity, infrastructure collapse, and large-scale dependence on humanitarian assistance.

Libya followed yet another trajectory, where the overthrow of Muammar Gaddafi in 2011 did not lead to stable reconstruction but instead to prolonged fragmentation. Competing militias, rival political authorities, and external interventions contributed to the breakdown of central governance. Control over territory and economic resources, particularly oil infrastructure, became divided among armed groups, resulting in shifting centres of power and persistent instability. Reporting by The Guardian in the years following the uprising consistently described Libya as a fragmented state in which institutional collapse allowed armed actors to dominate political and economic life.

Taken together, these trajectories raise a central question about the legacy of the Arab Spring. By the mid-2010s, it was increasingly evident that while the uprisings had exposed deep structural weaknesses in governance systems across the region, they had not produced stable political settlements in most countries. Scholars such as Marc Lynch have argued that the Arab uprisings represented a profound moment of political awakening that nevertheless struggled to generate sustainable institutional outcomes. Bruce Mutsvairo's work on digital journalism similarly highlights that while the uprisings temporarily expanded political expression and transformed media ecosystems, many states subsequently reasserted control over public discourse and curtailed media freedoms.

In retrospect, the Arab Spring appears less as a discrete historical episode and more as an ongoing political rupture. It demonstrated the capacity of mass mobilisation to challenge entrenched authoritarian systems, but also revealed the difficulty of transforming revolutionary energy into durable institutions without cohesive leadership, stable coalitions, and functioning state structures. Tunisia remains the closest example of partial democratic transition, though even its trajectory has faced significant reversals in later years. Elsewhere, outcomes ranged from renewed authoritarian consolidation to prolonged conflict and state fragmentation. What remains consistent across the region is that the uprisings exposed enduring demands for dignity, accountability, and economic justice, and those underlying pressures continue to shape political realities long after the initial wave of protests.

25 April, 2017

38

THE SULTAN IN ERDOGAN

TURKEY ENTERED A DECISIVE MOMENT IN 2017 as President Recep Tayyip Erdogan sought sweeping constitutional changes to transform the country's parliamentary system into an executive presidency. On 16 April, fifty-five million citizens were asked to vote on a package of 18 amendments. Reuters reported that the reforms abolished the office of prime minister, gave the president authority to appoint vice presidents and ministers without parliamentary approval, issue decrees, dissolve parliament under certain conditions, and exert influence over judicial appointments.

The BBC noted that the 'yes' camp narrowly prevailed with just over 51 per cent of the vote, a result that reconfigured Turkey's political architecture and allowed Erdogan to potentially remain in power until 2029. Supporters framed the reform as a path to stability, pointing to strong presidential systems in France and the United States.

Pro-government newspapers argued that coalition politics had paralysed Turkey for decades and that decisive executive authority was needed to confront terrorism and economic challenges.

Critics, however, saw the referendum as a power grab. The Financial Times warned that checks and balances would be weakened, while The Economist argued that Erdogan was positioning himself as an 'all-powerful sultan'. The Washington Post highlighted fears that the amendments would erode parliamentary oversight and judicial independence, leaving impeachment of a president nearly impossible.

The referendum came less than a year after the failed coup attempt of July 2016, which profoundly reshaped the state. The government declared a state of emergency that lasted almost two years. Amnesty International documented mass arrests and purges: around 40,000 people were detained, more than 100,000 public servants were dismissed, and 3,000 judges were removed. Erdogan's leadership attributed the coup plot to the network of exiled cleric Fethullah Gulen, once an ally but now accused of running a 'parallel state'. Gulen denied involvement, but the crackdown extended far beyond his followers. Human Rights Watch noted that journalists, academics, and opposition figures were swept up in prosecutions, often under broad anti-terror laws.

Press freedom deteriorated sharply. The Committee to Protect Journalists described Turkey as the world's leading jailer of journalists in 2016 and 2017. The newspaper Zaman was seized and placed under state control, while staff from Cumhuriyet were detained. Deutsche Welle reported that social media prosecutions became routine, with citizens jailed for tweets deemed insulting to the president. The New York Times observed that this climate of fear widened the gulf between Erdogan's supporters and secular, Kurdish, and liberal constituencies.

Erdogan's polarising image had already sharpened during the Gezi Park protests of 2013, when hundreds of thousands rallied against his paternalistic style of governance. CNN and the Guardian documented excessive police force, tear gas, and water cannons, as well as concerns about media censorship and limited public consultation. Protesters accused Erdogan of authoritarianism and disinformation.

The scars of Gezi lingered, especially among younger urban voters and minorities such as Alevis and Kurds, many of whom viewed the 2017 reform as consolidating executive dominance at their expense.

Security and the Kurdish question remained central. The armed conflict with the Kurdistan Workers' Party (PKK) intensified after the collapse of a peace process in 2015. Reuters reported on large-scale military operations in the southeast, curfews in Kurdish towns and the detention of elected mayors from the pro-Kurdish HDP. Erdogan's government treated the PKK's political wing as a terrorist entity, arguing that autonomy demands threatened national unity. Opposition figures warned that democratic pluralism was being eroded, while Al Jazeera noted that Kurdish grievances deepened as arrests mounted.

Foreign policy debates added further friction. In Syria, Turkey launched Operation Euphrates Shield in 2016, arguing that cross-border action was needed to push back ISIS and the YPG, which Ankara views as the Syrian branch of the PKK. The US military cooperated extensively with the YPG-led Syrian Democratic Forces against ISIS, a partnership that produced visible tension in US-Turkey relations. The Wall Street Journal reported on Ankara's insistence that Western support for the YPG undermined Turkish security. Erdogan himself accused the United States in December 2016 of supporting ISIS and Kurdish militias, claiming he had 'confirmed evidence with pictures and videos', a charge reported by outlets including Al Jazeera and Reuters. Washington strongly rejected the allegation, insisting it had never backed ISIS. Russian officials also accused Turkey of enabling ISIS oil smuggling in 2015, though Ankara rejected the claims. Independent investigations by major newspapers emphasised the complexity of smuggling networks and noted Turkey's subsequent military engagements against ISIS. Ahmet Sait Yayla, a former Turkish counter-terror chief, went further in interviews with investigative outlets such as INSURGE Intelligence and The Investigative Journal, and later in academic publications including Studies in Conflict & Terrorism and Perspectives on Terrorism, alleging that Turkish intelligence had facilitated ISIS operations through humanitarian relief agencies and tolerated smuggling networks. These claims remain disputed by Turkish authorities but illustrate the depth of controversy surrounding Ankara's regional role.

Economic undercurrents shaped public sentiment. Bloomberg reported that the lira depreciated sharply in 2016–2017, inflation rose, and tourism faltered after a series of terror attacks and the coup attempt. Erdogan's construction-driven growth model drew praise for infrastructure gains but criticism for patronage and debt risks. The lavish presidential complex in Ankara, reported by the Guardian to have cost more than half a billion dollars, became a symbol for opponents of alleged waste, while supporters framed it as fitting for a modernising state. Economic strains touched the middle class and poorer households, narrowing the government's room for manoeuvre and raising questions about whether an executive presidency could deliver stability without deeper reforms.

Inside the military and bureaucracy, Erdogan's consolidation accelerated after 2016. The purges, reorganisation of command structures, and reductions in the military's political influence were portrayed by pro-government media as the fulfilment of civilian supremacy, a long-standing goal since the era of military tutelage. The Economist argued that centralisation of appointments risked eroding institutional independence. Yayla's controversial assertions about state complicity with extremist networks added fuel to critics' arguments that Erdogan's consolidation was less about stability and more about shielding power.

The referendum campaign itself revealed how divided Turkey had become. Erdogan's allies argued in rallies covered by Anadolu Agency that executive leadership would break policy deadlocks and better confront security threats. Opposition leaders from the CHP and HDP warned that the amendments would dismantle checks and balances. International observers from the OSCE and Council of Europe raised concerns about media access, emergency-rule constraints, and allegations of irregularities, while Turkish authorities defended the legitimacy of the vote and rejected external criticism.

Looking ahead from 2017, analysts in the Financial Times suggested that the new system could keep Erdogan at the apex of power for an extended period, while also hard-wiring political polarisation. The Washington Post noted that Erdogan's core supporters, often in Anatolian provinces benefiting from infrastructure and social spending, embraced the changes as necessary for national strength. Minorities and secular urbanites tended to see the reforms as closing democratic space. Foreign Affairs and Brookings scholars warned that erosion of independent institutions would make future crises harder to manage and compromise investor confidence.

A balanced assessment recognises both the grievances driving calls for strong leadership and the dangers of overreach. Turkey faced real security threats, a traumatic coup attempt and geopolitical pressures that made executive decisiveness attractive to many voters. Yet enduring stability in complex societies typically requires credible institutions, judicial independence, press freedom and pluralist politics. The referendum delivered a political outcome but not necessarily a consensus. As Turkish newspapers across the spectrum reflected, the durability of the new order would depend on whether those wielding expanded powers could demonstrate restraint, rebuild trust and deliver results in the economy and security without silencing legitimate dissent.

In narrative terms, 2017 was a hinge year that reframed the state. It brought supporters the promise of a streamlined presidency and opponents the fear of entrenched dominance. It tethered domestic debates to regional conflicts and a shifting global order. And it left a question hanging over Turkish politics that observers in Reuters and BBC News repeatedly posed: can a system built to deliver stability avoid the pitfalls of hyper-centralisation, or will it exhaust the very social resilience it seeks to preserve?

17 April, 2017

39

ANARCHY IN SOUTH AFRICA

Economic disparities and corruption OFTEN make masses revolt, and South Africa, the so called rainbow nation, became the most recent country where public protests regained their course in April 2017. Since President Jacob Zuma assumed office in 2009, South Africa had witnessed numerous protests and demonstrations reflecting growing public dissatisfaction with corruption, inequality and government performance. The ANC, a 105 year old political party once chaired by Nelson Mandela, was facing internal revolts that threatened to fracture the organisation which had dominated the political scene since the end of apartheid in 1994. As Al Jazeera reported at the time, tens of thousands of South Africans poured into the streets in the largest demonstrations in years, demanding accountability and change.

President Jacob Zuma's decision to reshuffle key ministers and deputy ministers, many of whom were regarded as competent, triggered outrage. Critics argued that several replacements were politically loyal to Zuma and that the reshuffle had been undertaken without adequate consultation within the party. Opposition members drafted a no confidence vote against him, while the dismissal of Finance Minister Pravin Gordhan, widely acclaimed for his anti corruption stance, fuelled mass unrest.

Reuters noted that Gordhan's removal was seen as a direct attack on institutional integrity, with suspicions that Zuma acted under the influence of the Gupta business family, accused of offering bribes and manipulating state contracts. The Guardian reported that Gordhan had been praised internationally for stabilising the economy, and his dismissal was interpreted as a blow to investor confidence.

Zuma's reputation was plummeting, and he was increasingly viewed as corrupt and self serving due to a succession of controversial decisions accumulated over eight years in power. Many South Africans perceived his leadership as an assault on the poor, with frustrations and anger running high. Gordhan had already clashed with Zuma over management of the state treasury, attempting to root out nepotism in state owned companies.

He was also widely viewed as a restraint on expensive state projects, including the proposed nuclear expansion programme. The Financial Times observed that Gordhan's resistance to large scale spending plans symbolised a broader struggle between technocratic governance and Zuma's patronage politics.

In the post apartheid era, South Africans took to the streets demanding Zuma's resignation over corruption and economic decline. The rand fell sharply following the reshuffle, losing more than ten percent of its value against the US dollar over the period surrounding Gordhan's dismissal, while two credit rating agencies downgraded South African government debt to junk status. Food prices were rising due to inflation, compounding the hardship. The Constitutional Court had ruled against Zuma in a case involving millions spent on his private Nkandla residence, further damaging his credibility. The New York Times noted that Zuma's repeated violations of constitutional norms had eroded trust in the presidency.

Although Zuma defended his cabinet reshuffle as necessary, critics dismissed it as a political gimmick unlikely to bring effectiveness ahead of the 2019 elections.

Thousands of South Africans of all racial groups marched in Cape Town, Johannesburg, Durban and Pretoria to counter his populist rhetoric. Coalitions of civil groups such as Save South Africa Campaign, Outa, the Democratic Alliance and others contributed to the mass protests. Trade unions, business executives and members of the Communist Party joined in, while South Africans abroad, including in London, showed solidarity. Social media amplified the protests, with blogs and viral posts spreading images of placards and slogans. As IB Times UK reported, the demonstrations were among the most significant since the end of apartheid, uniting diverse communities in opposition to Zuma.

Protestors held blue placards, formed human chains, waved flags, danced and sang protest songs, while motorists raised fists in defiance. Many participants admitted they had never marched before, underscoring the extraordinary nature of the mobilisation. Nobel laureate Desmond Tutu, frail but resolute, joined the protests in Cape Town, lending moral authority to the movement. The government urged citizens not to opt for a national shutdown, and in some locations tensions escalated as confrontations occurred between pro Zuma supporters and anti Zuma demonstrators. Despite constitutional guarantees of the right to petition and peaceful assembly, the atmosphere was tense, with fears of escalation.

The ANC's history added poignancy to the crisis. The ANC, which was banned by the apartheid government in 1960, later adopted armed resistance through its military wing, Umkhonto we Sizwe. The party had produced leaders like Mandela and Zuma himself, who spent roughly a decade imprisoned by the apartheid government, much of it on Robben Island.

Zuma had played a role in organising ANC activities in

neighbouring countries and later rose through the party's ranks to become one of its most influential leaders. Yet by 2017, his legacy was overshadowed by allegations of corruption and betrayal of the movement's ideals. The Soweto uprising of 1976 had once symbolised resistance against apartheid, but now the protests of 2017 symbolised resistance against corruption within the liberation party itself.

Zuma insisted that western colonial mentality and white monopoly capitalism were behind efforts to oust him, framing the protests as externally driven. Yet the mass uprising told a different story. As Al Jazeera noted, ordinary South Africans from all social classes were demanding accountability, not foreign intervention. The protests revealed a society unwilling to tolerate corruption and economic mismanagement, even from a party that had delivered freedom. The Guardian observed that the ANC faced its gravest internal crisis since 1994, with the possibility of fracture looming.

By April 2017, South Africa stood at a crossroads. The protests were not merely about Zuma's cabinet reshuffle but about the broader trajectory of the nation. Economic disparities, corruption and patronage politics had eroded trust in institutions. The downgrade to junk status symbolised the economic consequences of political instability. The marches, uniting diverse communities, reflected a yearning for renewal. As Reuters reported, the protests were a warning that the ANC could no longer rely on its liberation legacy to secure loyalty. The people demanded integrity, accountability and leadership that served the public rather than personal interests.

Zuma's future was uncertain. He faced mounting pressure from opposition parties, civil society and even factions within the ANC.

The protests of April 2017 marked a turning point, showing that South Africans were prepared to defend democracy against corruption. Whether Zuma would step down or cling to power remained unresolved, but the uprising demonstrated that the rainbow nation's citizens were determined to hold leaders accountable. The legacy of Mandela and the sacrifices of the past demanded no less.

8 April, 2017

40

WAR IN YEMEN

W AR IN YEMEN WAS A RESULT OF a failed political transition, and by 2017 a resolution was becoming increasingly difficult. The uprising that had toppled Ali Abdullah Saleh in 2011 was supposed to usher in a new era of dialogue and reform, but the transition collapsed under the weight of factionalism, regional rivalries, and external interference. As the New York Times reported, the Houthis, a Zaydi Shia movement long marginalised, capitalised on discontent and expanded their influence, while the central government faltered. Saudi Arabia, meanwhile, saw Iranian expansionism in Shia centred areas of Yemen and Lebanon as a direct threat, and actively supported Sunni movements in the Arab world to counterbalance Tehran.

The Guardian noted that Riyadh's military budget had soared to $87 billion in 2016, the third largest globally, with US approved arms sales during the Obama administration and military aid from the United Kingdom bolstering its arsenal.

The Yemeni government was fighting Houthi rebels, whose movement emerged during the 1990s and whose armed insurgency against the government began in 2004, but the war escalated dangerously in recent years. The Houthis had already gained control of Saada province and neighbouring areas, and by 2014 they had entered Sana'a, Yemen's capital. The Washington Post described how common Yemenis, including Sunnis, initially supported the Houthis, seeing them as a force against corruption and neglect. By 2015, Houthi presence in the city was so strong that President Abd Rabbu Mansour Hadi fled to the southern port city of Aden for safety. Saudi Arabia then launched its intervention, supported by a coalition of Arab states, justifying its campaign by claiming the Houthis were Iranian proxies destabilising the region. In March 2017, Reuters reported that Iran backed arms shipments to the Houthis were intercepted, reinforcing Saudi claims of active connections between Tehran and Houthi leaders.

The humanitarian toll was catastrophic. Seventy per cent of Yemen's population needed aid, and the UN warned that the conflict was causing mounting civilian deaths and pushing millions towards famine. The BBC placed Yemen firmly on the global radar, describing starvation as imminent. Western Yemen was largely under Houthi control, while the city of Taiz remained a fiercely contested battleground where rebels fired missiles in retaliation. Journalists from Associated Press reported that sniper fire in Taiz struck indiscriminately, with children among the victims, and that landmines had been planted randomly. Hospitals were overwhelmed, and treatment was impossible. Access for reporters was rare and dangerous, with the Guardian noting that bodies lay in the open as fighting raged.

The Yemeni government, backed by the UK, US and France, managed to drive rebels out of Aden to secure pro government leaders. Yet the chaos allowed ISIS militants to exploit the vacuum. The Independent reported that ISIS fighters stepped up attacks in Aden, bombing Zaydi Shia mosques and spreading terror. Infrastructure across Yemen was reduced to rubble. As the Financial Times observed, being the Arab world's poorest country, Yemen faced decades of recovery even under normalisation. More than ten thousand people had been killed by 2017, including thousands of civilians, and aid agencies warned that more would perish from hunger. Yemen relied on imports for 90 per cent of its food, but blockades imposed since April 2015 and aerial bombardments made survival precarious. Al Jazeera documented how Saudi airstrikes hit schools, health facilities and wedding parties, while Amnesty International charged the coalition with using cluster munitions banned in over 100 countries.

Attempts at reconciliation had failed. In 2013, a national dialogue conference was launched, and although the Houthis participated in the process, they later rejected key aspects of the political settlement, contributing to the collapse of the transition. By 2014–15 the process had unravelled completely. Saudi backed forces and coalition partners struggled to achieve their aims, and the coalition's objectives remained elusive. The UN reported that tens of thousands of Yemenis had fled to Somalia and Djibouti, where they faced inadequate shelter and food shortages. The Guardian highlighted how Yemeni culture viewed invaders with disdain, recalling that Ottoman Turks and Egyptians had both failed to subdue the country despite superior numbers and armour. This historical memory fuelled resistance to the Saudi led coalition.

Saudi Arabia's campaign drew comparisons with the US invasion of Afghanistan. The Washington Post noted that despite trillions of dollars spent and advanced weaponry, the US had not defeated the Taliban. Observers asked how Riyadh could expect to defeat the Houthis, who controlled sizeable territory and enjoyed local support. By 2017, Saudi forces were still struggling to secure their southern border with Yemen, facing cross border raids and missile attacks. The New York Times reported that the US was unlikely to restrain Saudi Arabia from continuing its military campaign, and the Trump administration signalled deeper military involvement. Meanwhile, no world leader was attempting to solve Yemen's food crisis, leaving millions at risk of famine.

The war in Yemen by 2017 had become a microcosm of regional rivalries. Saudi Arabia framed its intervention as a bulwark against Iranian expansion, while Iran denied direct control but was accused of supplying arms and training. The Guardian described Yemen as a battlefield where proxy dynamics played out, with ordinary civilians bearing the brunt. The humanitarian crisis was labelled by the UN as the worst in the world, with cholera outbreaks compounding starvation. Journalists such as Patrick Cockburn in the Independent argued that Yemen illustrated the futility of external military solutions in deeply fractured societies. The Economist warned that the longer the war continued, the more entrenched the Houthis became, and the more radicalised the population risked becoming.

By 2017, Yemen's war was not only a domestic struggle but a regional confrontation, a humanitarian disaster, and a test of international resolve. The collapse of political transition had opened the gates to chaos, and the Saudi led coalition's intervention had deepened the crisis. The Houthis controlled large swathes of territory, ISIS exploited instability, and millions faced hunger. The New York Times concluded that Yemen's tragedy was a reminder that failed transitions can spiral into wars that defy resolution. Unless genuine dialogue was revived and humanitarian aid prioritised, Yemen risked becoming a permanent scar on the Arab world's conscience.

31 March, 2017

41

CPEC: A GAME CHANGER

CHINA HAS BEEN PAKISTAN'S NUMBER ONE FRIEND, for several reasons, under the current strategic context. It is not only extending its military and political backing but is also willing to lend a push to the economic environment.

CPEC is a mega-project investment and is perhaps the biggest of its kind in the region. The assistance is bigger than what the United States has given Pakistan, since 2002.

The corridor has been in the news, for all the right and wrong reasons. It is yet again showing that Islamabad is getting closer to Beijing, and its alliance with Washington is slowly declining.

Infrastructure development capabilities, and harnessing the potential of Pakistan's natural reserves will strengthen CPEC goals, but lack of transparency in their financial agenda has recently caused retaliatory attacks.

Economic experts believe that it will add immense economic activity, inside Pakistan, including the construction of special economic zones, pipeline ventures, road works, telecom projects, internet technology-based projects, rail works, social sector development projects, and renewable energy projects.

China, on the other hand, believes in reaping the benefits,

of this agreement, by quicker availability of energy resources, via Pakistan, from the Middle East, by avoiding the Malacca Strait, and the South China Sea.

The CPEC project investment is intra-Pakistan in nature that is targeting income-generating sectors.

Projects have been identified in transit routes across the country. It starts from Xinjiang in China, passes from the Gilgit-Baltistan region, in the north of Pakistan, and will extent up to Gwadar port in the south. 54$ billion is the current investment plan for the development corridor. About 19 million tonnes of crude oil will be directly transferred to China, through Gwadar. 17,000 megawatts of electricity will be produced. To add to that, China will have a shorter route to enter African, West Asian, and South Asian trade, where already a huge number of Chinese entrepreneurs, and workers are based.

On the CPEC website (www.cpec.gov.pk), about sixty-seven working projects have been cited. The Pakistani government believes that the framework, on which the investment project is designed, will have a positive impact on Iran, Afghanistan, India, and Central Asian Republics. And, CPEC also claims to enhance academic, cultural, regional knowledge, and transfer of human capital and services.

While Pakistan's current electricity generation fulfils the domestic requirement, more production can likely be used to sell electricity, and improve circular debts. The project already has gained hostility in the Balochistan region, which has weak relations with the central government. *Balochi* activists also fear the influx of non-Balochis in the region. This has prompted the Pakistani government to increase the security network in the region. Already, special forces are being deployed in the Balochistan region, to protect the newly constructed super highways. On the other hand, a stronger relationship with Gilgit Baltistan region from the centre will likely be expected, in the coming time. So clearly, there have been regional political implications affecting the investment scenario, inside Pakistan, courtesy of China. Some of the regional politicians in Pakistan are already criticising the project because it does not pass through their areas. This aloofness can even lead to civil discontent, because CPEC has promised 700,000 direct jobs, till 2030.

CPEC also remains vulnerable to terrorist attacks. Xinjiang is home to Uyghur Muslims and is a breeding ground for a separatist movement. China has been repeatedly blaming the Uighur extremists, for the recent surge of violence.

In the past, NATO supplies passing through Pakistan have also been targeted by the Taliban. So, Pakistan and China need to make no stone unturned, in designing a robust security plan. Troops are already being recruited to protect Chinese workers, and enterprises, on the corridor, but more needs to be done.

The corridor is currently being marketed, as a win - win situation, for both countries. Pakistan has the potential to become a direct beneficiary of China's manufacturing sector, while China can also benefit from the agricultural, and aqua sectors of Pakistan. Only time can decide which country would benefit more, in the longer term.

Pakistan is aiming to become an upper middle-income economy, by 2025, but, India, is unhappy with the Chinese-funded project because it passes through the Pakistani-administered Kashmir.

Hence, CPEC is beginning to change the power dynamics in the SAARC arena, as well.

Kashmiri nationalists are already opposing the CPEC. It will also strain the existing Indo-China relationship. Also, the Chinese, still make an active presence, in the Gilgit Baltistan region.

17 March, 2017

42

BREWING OF AMERICAN POLITICS

Don't get carried over by eloquent speeches and joy. It is false propaganda. These are acts to appease those in the halls of power and a fool's game. The critiques of Barack Obama have hit hard, with an accuracy of their facts that most people did not even care to read about.

American 'interventions' have been made in our world for wars, and butchering large human populations. The only difference between Bush and Obama was that Bush was more vocal and clearer, about what he wanted to do.

There was a time when ardent followers of Barack Obama did not like his critiques. He, on the contrary, was a techno-fascist military strategist, disguised as a Nobel Peace Laureate, operated by Wall Street, corporate America, and the Pentagon. He defined the idiocy of the right, and the pandering platitudes of a dictator, only through a sustained, and massive democratic movement.

Dumping political anger is not democracy. Ironic, it may seem, but the recent shift of power from Democrats to Republicans will keep the political dogma, of arrogance and ignorance, intact.

Both political centres represent the same side of the coin, and Republicans in power, are giving rise to new developments, including a comprehensive register of

Muslims, a travel ban from selected Islamic countries, and a new law where refugees will not be entertained. It seems the radicalisation of American politics is very much part of the Republican plan. They have their tails up for it.

Immigration now will be a racial discourse. Religion will divide people. Judges will be used as pawns. Laws and courts will compete with nationalism. Huge military build-ups are new promises. Political satires on the Swedish Government, and attacking journalistic freedom of respected and objective media houses in the world, such as *Al-Jazeera*, by the new American President Donald Trump, will keep controversies intact. Political apathy is poisonous. His irate leadership, dragged by immaturity, will bring defeat to statesmanship but he does not seem to care.

The same policies will be followed to contain the Middle East, for national interests: to fund the nepotism and corruption of monarchies, militarism, client political parties, and groups, and to economically deprive its common countrymen. More power and freedom will be given to Israel, to pursue its expansionist policies. Two State solution is long dead. Most Palestinians are still refugees, and Israel wants more land. But, Americans, still trying to sort out a productive bargain, for both parties involved, is an obnoxious cause, that too in an environment of imposing stringent sanctions, and undertaking military actions, whenever they please.

The nature of politics is often unforeseen, and full of farce, due to dreamy possibilities. Some undisputed facts are also accumulating, involving active Russian connections with Trump's three main campaigners, for defeating the Democrats, in the last election. Russia, is, in fact, a country, with which Americans have a cold war. Trump also had several financial dealings with Russian oligarchs, in the past, when he headed his business empire. His political perceptions are also somewhat the same because he wants to give more power to people, who own America, and influence common American lives, economically.

Elites are hated when inequalities tend to grow. And, if Trump wants to pursue politics, as an entrepreneurial agenda, to guarantee electoral security, to his party members, and himself then promised motives of serving a republic will altogether be wasted. The satisfaction of a selective public is not a primal example of good leadership. All this is happening at a time when common Americans want to occupy Wall Street.

The new state has been given full access to abuse anonymity of their intelligence services, as well. His administration also does not fear state protests. Some of these revolts against the new government have already been posted on media that reflect cultural disintegration, in the American community.

There have been long marches of people holding placards and riots. Several cars have been burned cars in downtown streets. Protestors have had confrontations with the police. It is in these places, where Trump is despised and derided. It reflects that many Americans are not happy with their new president.

The American government also cannot use their policeman whip to instil their version of democracy anymore, against the world having a wave of stern resistance, under the pretext of their foreign policy.

The truth is as hard to swallow, as it is to speak. We are heading to a dangerous new world, full of uncertainties.

Their single presidential execution harbouring nukes can ruin the world order.

26 February, 2017

43

RUSSIA'S ENVIRONMENTAL CONFLICTS

M AN IS IN A CONFLICT WITH NATURE. 2015 has been recorded as the hottest year in world history. Climate change is happening right now, and countries like Russia should put it high on their agenda, because it has the world's largest reserves of forests, and is a sanctuary of over one hundred twenty thousand rivers, and two million lakes.

Global warming will affect Russia more than other countries. Russian climatologists suggest that climate change is affecting Russia, 30% faster than other countries.

Issues, such as giant methane holes, intense snow melt floods, and extreme weather events, that have been predicted by the Federal Environment, Ministry of Russia, will likely bring construction challenges.

The energy sector will also likely suffer. For example, power cuts will make poor people suffer more, who belong to the colder regions, and it can also complicate migration policies.

For a while, Russian scientists had been denying the existence of climate change. To rebut their claims, very recently, Greenpeace campaigners in Moscow were demanding the awareness of climate change, high on the agenda, for the public domain.

On a political level though, after the Copenhagen

Conference held in 2009, climate change has been in 'some kind of operation,' but has not been implemented quite well.

Many analysts say that Russia is contradicting its climate change commitments for not giving general subsidies to produce fossil fuels.

Scholarly perceptions of Russia's environmental problems are limited. On March 2015, Russia became one of the first countries to submit its 'nationally determined contributions,' under the United Nations Framework on Climate Change (UNFCCC).

Russia announced that it would reduce its carbon emissions by up to 25-30%, by the year 2030. Ten years ago, it also signed the Kyoto Protocol – a multilateral agreement to reduce at least 5% emissions.

But these developments are causing controversy, because Russia still is one of the largest carbon-intensive economies in the world. From the year 1990 to 2005, Russia failed to keep up with its emission targets.

Russia's weak climate change policy is due to several factors which include: prioritisation of economic development over environment protection, close ties between the state and energy sector, lack of clarity in the legal environment, widespread corruption, weak environment institutions, and low level of awareness, and concern in the public domain.

Currently, problems of nuclear waste, deforestation and pollution are largely going unnoticed.

It brings Russia to the top of the world's deforestation

charts, from 2000 to 2012, having lost a forest area, equal to Switzerland. It has the greatest number of polluted cities that are largely attributed to its industry.
Volga River, which also flows through Europe, remains one of the most polluted, and the problem is directly linked to economic developments.

In southern Siberia, farms are dying, trees are felled, and people are leaving. There are tales from these Russian villages, where government administration has failed to keep up its promise, to deliver gas, in all parts of the region.

There are no social programmes, and unemployment is on the increase. Commodities are imported from Turkey and Israel because that makes them cheaper than building warehouses. There is also a need for investments in agriculture.

One of the greatest problems for indigenous people has also been the network of pipes, and plants, that pass through the regions, where people live. Climate change is affecting traditional ways of life, and threatening communities. There is a conflict between indigenous peoples and mining companies.

In Bashkortostan, which lies just south of the Ural Mountains, there is a heated tussle going on between Russia's largest chemical consortia, and the local population. For them, the hills are sacred, and are a ritual site for certain local tribes, like the *Yurmat*.

Therefore, it seems that some special decisions need to be taken, in this tug-of-war. Public opinion is against these developments.

For indigenous people, like the *Shors*, coal mining means

the loss of ancestral land, traditional crafts, and ways of life. Residents have also been forced to sell their houses and leave.

Many are also concerned about public health. Very rarely, do mining companies receive a license, after environmental advice.

However, the biggest challenge has been the unpredictability of the weather. There has been a decline in snow, an increase in flooding, and the destruction of the shores of certain rivers, and lakes, which are causing enormous environmental conflicts, across the region.

10 March, 2016

44

WAR IN SYRIAN TERRITORIES

SYRIA'S WAR HAS BEEN ONE OF the most destructive conflicts of the twenty-first century. By 2013, the Assad regime was already regaining ground in Latakia against rebels, but it was not until September 2015 that Russia formally launched its air campaign in Syria. As BBC News reported, Moscow's intervention marked a turning point, enabling Assad's forces to recapture rebel-held areas with Russian air power and military support.

The Syrian army, supported by Hezbollah and Iranian-backed militias, pushed northwards towards the Turkish border, raising tensions with Ankara.

As Reuters reported, the Russian Foreign Ministry in February 2016 insisted it had "not received convincing evidence of civilian deaths" from its strikes. Humanitarian organisations, monitoring groups, and journalists, however, documented numerous incidents involving civilian casualties. Al Jazeera journalist Ibrahim al-Omar was killed in July 2016 while reporting in Idlib Province; Al Jazeera stated that he died in a suspected Russian airstrike.

Three actors—the Kurds, Assad's loyalists, and Turkey—were central to the war's shifting dynamics. The United States combined military involvement with diplomatic efforts aimed at achieving a political settlement, but its influence waned as Russia expanded its role in the conflict. Following Russia's annexation of Crimea and the deterioration of relations between Moscow and Western governments, some commentators described Syria as part of a broader geopolitical rivalry between Russia and NATO powers.

Turkey meanwhile feared direct confrontation with Moscow over developments in Aleppo and Latakia. Many other reporters from Al Jazeera narrowly survived suspected Russian airstrikes in Idlib while covering civilian casualties, underscoring the dangers of Moscow's campaign.

Turkey's role was controversial. Some analysts argued that Ankara's early border policies and prioritisation of containing Kurdish armed groups created conditions from which ISIS indirectly benefited, a claim consistently rejected by Turkish authorities.

The siege of Kobani in 2014–15, described by PBS Frontline and CNN's Ben Wedeman, saw ISIS capture numerous surrounding villages, commit serious abuses against civilians, and force large-scale displacement. The Kurdish YPG, with US air support, eventually recaptured the city, but much of it was destroyed, as BBC correspondents confirmed.

Syria's Kurdish population, estimated at between two and three million people before the war, sought autonomy in a region many Kurdish activists call "Rojava". They divided their territory into three cantons, promoting secularism and gender equality. The Democratic Union Party (PYD) and its armed wing, the YPG, ran local administrations, broadcasting Kurdish cultural programmes on television and radio. Schools and salaries remained funded by Damascus, but Kurdish militias controlled daily life. Scholars such as Vittoria Federici in *The Rise of Rojava* noted that the Syrian army's partial withdrawal in 2012 allowed Kurdish militias to consolidate control.

ISIS retaliated with car bombs and suicide attacks, destabilising Rojava. Yet the Kurds took pride in their secular institutions and egalitarian ethos. Russia later expanded its presence around Qamishli as part of broader efforts to strengthen its influence in northeastern Syria. Russia also participated in ceasefire negotiations and local reconciliation arrangements involving government and opposition forces. Christoph Reuter of *Der Spiegel* emphasised that Assad's battlefield successes since 2015 were not due to his weakened army but to Russian air power, Hezbollah, and Iranian-backed militias from Iraq and Afghanistan.

The Kurds maintained relations with both the United States and Russia. With US air support, they fought Daesh while also engaging Moscow. Saudi Arabia joined the coalition against ISIS, aligning with Washington. This manoeuvring unsettled Ankara, where anti-Kurdish sentiment ran deep. Peace talks in Riyadh between the Syrian government and opposition excluded the Kurds, reflecting Turkish pressure. Journalists from *The Guardian* noted that Ankara regarded Kurdish autonomy in northern Syria as a major security concern, shaping its diplomatic stance.

Turkey, in 2016, as a strategic and security measure, demanded a no-fly zone from Jarabulus to Azaz, the same area the Kurds sought to seize from ISIS. Turkish officials argued the zone would protect civilians from Assad's air force. The Kurds saw it as a pretext for Turkey to bomb YPG fighters. Ankara's opposition to Kurdish separatism and autonomy movements was longstanding.

With time, Turkish artillery support in Aleppo and Latakia failed strategically, as Assad's army and Hezbollah fighters held firm. By February 2016, Turkish armoured vehicles were entrenched along the border, building trenches and concrete walls, as Reuters correspondents observed.

Turkey also provided support to various anti-Damascus opposition factions, including groups that later became associated with Turkish-backed formations in northern Syria.

Christoph Reuter of *Spiegel Online* reported that Assad's victories since 2015 were sustained by Russian air power and foreign militias rather than domestic strength. The United States, once focused on toppling Assad, shifted to dismantling ISIS. With 2,000 troops in eastern Syria working with the Syrian Democratic Forces, Washington lacked the diplomatic capacity to shape peace. Israel, on the other hand, used the conflict to intensify strikes against Iranian-linked targets, launching hundreds of airstrikes to prevent weapons transfers to Hezbollah. Reuters reported that Israel intensified strikes against what it described as Iranian-linked targets in Syria, while Syrian authorities reported civilian casualties in some incidents. Israeli operations periodically targeted military facilities and infrastructure in and around Damascus as part of efforts to limit Iran's military presence in Syria.

Civilians withstood the worst of the conflict. In Jisr al-Shughur, one of the first battlegrounds, families sold homes and furniture to escape. Many fled with only what could fit on motorcycles or cars, as jets roared overhead. Medicines were transported through hostile territory from Damascus, and civil aviation remained under regime control.

The Syrian Observatory for Human Rights estimated that by 2018 more than 360,000 people had died, while later estimates placed the death toll above 500,000. Filippo Grandi, the United Nations High Commissioner for Refugees, warned that renewed fighting in Idlib could trigger mass displacement, echoing concerns raised by UN News.

The Kurds' exclusion from peace talks underscored their precarious position. Ankara viewed Kurdish autonomy along its southern border as a major security concern, and its opposition contributed to the exclusion of Kurdish representatives from some negotiations. The Kurds, however, continued to promote secularism and gender equality, distinguishing themselves from Islamist factions. Journalists such as Gayle Tzemach Lemmon, writing for the Council on Foreign Relations, highlighted the extraordinary role of Kurdish women fighters in resisting ISIS.

Ultimately, Syria's war reflected the interplay of global powers. Russia sought to secure Assad's regime and expand its influence in the Middle East at a time of heightened tensions with Western powers. Turkey manoeuvred to contain the Kurds while supporting rebels. The United States shifted focus to ISIS, abandoning broader ambitions. Israel struck Iranian targets, while Iran entrenched militias. The Kurds balanced between Washington and Moscow, seeking autonomy but facing hostility from Ankara. As Al Jazeera concluded, only a coherent peace process could stabilise Syria. Yet with fragmented opposition, entrenched foreign powers, and deep mistrust, peace remained elusive.

The war weariness of Syrians was palpable, but the politics of the region continued to be shaped by external actors. Without compromise, Syria remained vulnerable to the influence of competing regional and international powers, with civilians continuing to pay the highest price.

19 February, 2016

45

TRAGEDY OF GREEK DEBTS

THERE IS CLAMOUR IN GREECE, about the Tsipras administration, doing mere lip service, on economic changes, which they loathed in their election rallies after the mandate supported them.

In July, 2015, the bailout programme was defended by Tspiras and it must go well with the hopes of the Greek public.

But there has been no real enthusiasm shown for tax reforms. Rather, there has been a tax surge. More than 60,000 Greek farmers have been asked to pay additional taxes, and pre-pay at least fifty per cent, of next year's tax. Some 70,000 businesses must pay a hundred per cent tax, for next year, in advance. Every service employee, in government service, will have pension cutbacks.

Greek leaders do not only need a credible strategy, which will drive them out of debt, but they also got to have an eye on their public expenditure.

Most of the Greek bonds have been sold off by international banks and foreign investors, which means, that these institutions are no longer responsible, for what happens in the Greek economy.

Greece came into crisis, after Wall Street, had a slump in 2008. There was an outcry about the soundness of the Greek finances, in 2009, and as a result, Greece was thrown out of the lending business. By the end of 2010, it had announced bankruptcy.

To avert the economic dangers, the so-called troika, the International Monetary Fund, the European Central Bank, and European Commission issued bailouts, for about 240 billion Euros. However, these bailouts came at a price, which forced the leaders to impose harsh austerity measures, requiring budget cuts, and tax increases.

There also have been stories of tax evasion, corruption, and oligarchic habits plummeting the Greek economic system. However, the mockery, by the banks, and investors, has been to get something in return, under punitive conditions, thereby showing the pawns of vicious capitalism, the world has been plunged into.

But, as observers, one might ask: why is Greece suffering even after the release of bailout funds? The truth lies elsewhere.

Most of the finances, that the country received, have gone into paying off its loans, rather than making its way into the economy. Healthcare is one of the worst-hit public sectors, in the country. There have been cases where even cancer patients have been denied treatment.

There are harsh capital controls, with long queues on the automated teller cash machines with a limit of sixty Euros a day. As the result, the country still has a huge debt load, and unemployment has risen to twenty-five per cent.

Dozens of Alexis Tsipras's elected members, of his left-wing Syriza party, have refused to back Greece's third bailout package, and about twenty-five per cent, of far-left dissidents, in his party, have formed the third biggest group, called the 'Popular Unity.'

Greeks even have shown their further mistrust, in politics, by presenting a low voter turnout, which was below 57%, even one polling station in Athens reporting only twenty-five voters, during three hours period.

Migrant crises from the Middle East were another problem that affected the voting, in the last election. About three people died in anti-austerity protests, in Syntagma Square, in April 2010, when a petrol bomb was thrown, into a nearby bank. In April 2012, a retired pharmacist, living on a pension, shot and killed himself, and blamed the act on the government.

Recent problems associated with the Euro currency, have also implied certain economists, to raise questions, about its membership, with the Eurozone.

The main problem with the Euro has been the recent ease of the Growth and Stability pact, which has left the currency with an uncertain management structure, made up of the European Bank, the Commission, and individual governments, all having an independent influence. If there are no productive formal relations, between these institutions, then what is the point of power autonomy in the first place?

So, if by any chance, Greece left the Eurozone, what is known as *'Grexit,'* many policy makers believe that it would not be such a catastrophe. Many still believe that if the country pulls out of the EU, it would fare much better.

Greeks have taken to social media to express their foment on the crises. According to them, these deals have no social conscience. Many citizens have voted against these bailouts, which they believe, will have dire consequences for the common masses.

11 October, 2015

46

IN SEARCH OF HOME

AT THE HEART OF THE MIGRANT CRISES of our age lies a dangerous convergence of power and division, where political ambition hardens into dogma and dogma into fanaticism. The greatest burden falls not on those who wield power, but on families stripped of home, heritage, and belonging. Their journeys—fraught with uncertainty—demand resilience, hope, and often sheer luck to secure even the most basic sustenance. As The Guardian observed, 'the refugee crisis is not only about numbers but about human dignity and survival.'

Recent conflicts have produced displacement on a staggering scale, with violence in Iraq's Ramadi alone forcing millions from their homes. Since the beginning of 2014, fighting displaced about 2.8 million Iraqis, according to UN figures reported by BBC News. In 2013, about 40,000 South Sudanese were waiting to be transported from Sudan, where they lived in appalling conditions in Khartoum squatter camps. The Office for the Coordination of Humanitarian Affairs estimated that this operation required at least $20 million, highlighting the scale of logistical and financial challenges. The New York Times noted that 'South Sudan's independence did not end the suffering of its people, many of whom remain stranded in limbo.'

Humanitarian systems, already strained, have struggled to meet even the most basic needs, leaving thousands exposed to hunger and deprivation. The UN World Food Programme reported in 2014 that there was not enough food to feed at least 30,000 displaced Iraqis for a month in Qamishli. Around three million people remained in hard-to-reach areas, including 242,000 in besieged zones without humanitarian access. Human Rights Watch emphasised that 'starvation is being used as a weapon of war,' underscoring the deliberate denial of aid.

What were once temporary shelters have, in many cases, evolved into permanent urban realities, reflecting the protracted nature of displacement. Zaatari refugee camp in Jordan has grown from a town of tents into a bustling city hosting at least 81,000 Syrians, making it the ninth largest city in Jordan. Over 20,000 also live in the newer Azraq camp, while others struggle in urban areas with UN cash assistance. The Washington Post described Zaatari as 'a city of exile, where children grow up knowing only displacement.'

State responses to migration have often compounded human suffering rather than alleviating it, as deportation policies disregard the vulnerability of those affected. Saudi Arabia deported 12,000 Somali migrants in 2014, a move criticised by Human Rights Watch. The International Organisation for Migration said Saudi Arabia planned to deport another 30,000 Somalis in its campaign against undocumented workers. Al Jazeera reported that 'the deportations risk sending vulnerable people back into conflict zones.'

For many, the journey itself becomes a deadly gamble, where the search for safety is overshadowed by the risk of death. At least 42 African migrants drowned off Yemen's southern coast in 2014. The International Organisation for Migration estimated that 7,000 migrants died at sea in 2013 while seeking safe havens. Between 2,000 and 5,000 Africans perished crossing the Sinai Peninsula to Israel or the Gulf of Aden to Yemen. The Guardian wrote that 'the

Mediterranean has become the world's deadliest border.'

Sectarian violence has further deepened the crisis, forcing communities into flight along lines of identity and faith. Sectarian violence in the Central African Republic killed thousands in 2013. The UN evacuated nearly 100 Muslims from Bangui to Bambari, 300 kilometres from the capital. Reuters reported that 'the exodus of Muslims from CAR is a sign of deepening sectarian division.'

Europe's southern frontier has emerged as a focal point of the crisis, with thousands risking perilous sea crossings in search of refuge. To reach Italy in an attempt, about 170,000 migrants arrived by sea in 2014, while 3,500 perished during the journey. Italian coastguards and merchant ships rescued thousands from overcrowded boats near Libya. In April alone, 1,500 were picked up from five boats. Mediterranean deaths, especially in the Channel of Sicily, surpassed 2,000 that year. The Financial Times observed that 'Europe's southern shores have become the frontline of a humanitarian emergency.'

The influx of migrants has placed immense strain on European states, exposing fractures in collective responsibility. Italy and Greece struggled to cope with arrivals. Austria stopped accepting asylum requests to pressure other European nations, as asylum applications rose by 160 percent. The New York Times reported that Austria demanded a fixed quota scheme to share responsibility.

On the margins of Europe, desperation has given rise to makeshift worlds of waiting and uncertainty. Around 3,000 migrants lived near the Eurotunnel between France and Britain in a makeshift camp known as 'the jungle', trying nightly to board trucks to reach the UK without permits. The Guardian described the camp as 'a symbol of

Europe's failure to manage migration humanely.'

National policies have increasingly tilted towards restriction rather than refuge, as governments grapple with political and security pressures. Turkey introduced strict measures to tackle the influx from Syria, citing fighting between Kurds and Daesh.

Israel, on the other hand, rejected calls to accept Syrian refugees, although it had previously hosted several refugees from Darfur, reflecting a more selective humanitarian engagement. Social media erupted when the body of a young boy was found on a Turkish beach, a tragedy that BBC News said 'shocked the world into recognising the human cost of the refugee crisis.'

Amid this landscape, Germany briefly stood apart with a more open approach, positioning itself as a principal destination for asylum seekers. Germany recorded at least 300,000 asylum seekers in 2015, becoming a leading destination due to its economic strength. Spain also pledged to do more. The Economist noted that 'Germany's openness contrasted with the reluctance of other EU states.'

Yet across regions, reluctance and resistance have often overshadowed solidarity, as states prioritise domestic concerns over humanitarian obligations. Amnesty International argued that countries like Turkey, Lebanon, and Jordan deliberately closed borders due to economic strain, pushing people back into conflict in violation of international obligations. Hungary expressed fears of becoming a minority nation amid the crisis. The Guardian reported that 'Hungary's rhetoric reflects deeper anxieties about identity and sovereignty.'

Efforts at collective European action have remained

tentative and contested, reflecting the difficulty of forging consensus. In June 2015, the EU agreed to relocate at least 40,000 refugees from Italy and Greece over two years, mostly Syrians and Iraqis. This replaced unpopular quotas. Overall, migration by land and sea jumped 149 percent. Reuters noted that 'the EU's relocation plan was a compromise, but implementation remained slow and contested.'

Taken together, these developments reveal a crisis shaped as much by political failure as by human tragedy. The refugee crisis reveals the intersection of war, poverty, and political failure. From Ramadi to Khartoum, Zaatari to the Mediterranean, millions have been uprooted. Their plight exposes the inadequacy of international responses. Camps intended as temporary shelters have become permanent cities.

It has been also observed that wealthier nations often resist responsibility, while poorer neighbours' shoulder disproportionate burdens. Germany's acceptance of hundreds of thousands of asylum seekers was praised as humanitarian, but it also fuelled political backlash domestically. Hungary's fears of demographic change illustrate how migration challenges national identity as much as it strains resources.

Nowhere is the human cost starker than at sea, where hope and despair converge in fatal crossings. The Mediterranean has become a graveyard, and the tragedy of the young Syrian boy found on a Turkish beach became a symbol of global indifference. Yet despite public outrage, policy responses remain piecemeal. The EU's relocation plan was slow and contested, revealing the gap between rhetoric and action. Economic dimensions are equally important. Refugees are often portrayed as burdens, yet studies cited by Financial Times show that migrants contribute to growth when integrated effectively. Germany's labour market absorbed many Syrians, while Spain argued for doing more to harness refugee potential. Conversely, deportations from Saudi Arabia highlight how economic campaigns against undocumented workers can worsen humanitarian crises.

Equally troubling is the erosion of the legal frameworks meant to protect the displaced, as states increasingly sidestep their obligations. The crisis also exposes the fragility of international law. The 1951 Refugee Convention obliges states to protect those fleeing persecution, yet Amnesty International has documented widespread violations, from border closures to forced returns. Political calculations often override legal commitments. Austria's suspension of asylum requests in 2015 was intended to pressure other EU states, but it undermined the principle of shared responsibility.

Ultimately, beyond statistics and policy debates, this is a question of dignity, of lives disrupted and futures denied. At its core, displacement is about human dignity. Families uprooted from Ramadi, Khartoum or Bangui are not statistics but people deprived of home, culture, and security. As The Washington Post wrote of Zaatari, 'children are growing up knowing only exile.' The long-term consequences are profound: generations raised without stable education, healthcare or citizenship risk becoming permanently marginalised, fuelling cycles of poverty and instability.

The refugee crisis thus stands as both a humanitarian emergency and a political reckoning, testing the limits of global cooperation and moral responsibility. The refugee crisis is therefore both humanitarian and political. It challenges the capacity of states, the solidarity of international institutions, and the conscience of societies.

The Guardian concluded that 'the refugee crisis is not a temporary emergency but a defining challenge of our age.'

Unless structural causes — war, poverty, persecution — are addressed alongside fairer burden sharing, the crisis will persist. Refugees will continue to risk their lives at sea, camps will swell into cities, and political divisions will deepen.

22 October, 2015

47

RISE OF BRICS NATIONS

WORLD'S FOUR EMERGING ECONOMIES Brazil, Russia, India, and China are poised to become the leading global economies, in the twenty-first century.

China's decade of unprecedented growth has eclipsed Japan, as the world's second-largest economy. Brazil has harnessed its resources and has become the largest economy, in Latin America. India will soon become the most populated country, in the world, with a young and educated work force. Russia, for a while, has dominated its position, as the world's leading energy supplier.

Recent economic data, on foreign direct investments, both to and from, these developing countries, reflect the appearance of the rise of a new economic bloc, on the world stage.

FDI outflows from BRICS states accounted for $146 billion, in 2011. This is almost 10 per cent of the world's GDP output, shared by four developing countries.

World Investment Report (2012) ascertains that outward FDI from developing nations, by 'Third World Multinationals,' is globalising at a faster rate, than its western counterparts.

In economic theory, outward FDI helps in productivity improvements, linked to increased specialisation of firms, competing in international markets, as well as the transfer of technology and knowledge. There are also location and ownership advantages. So, the internationalisation of third-world corporations is beneficial.

That is why, David Collins, a senior lecturer at City University London suggested that corporations, from the third world, now make up their presence, in the world's largest 500 global firms. For example, Brazil's *Andrade Gutierrez* and Russia's *Sistema* are rising players in the global construction and telecommunication sectors. Indian and Chinese companies have been recently involved in requisitions of western firms: *Dr Reddy's*, an Indian pharmaceutical, and China's *Unicom*, a telecommunication giant.

Modified technology transfers, according to local cultures and tastes, have given many local companies, from BRICS states, a competitive edge, over their competitors in markets, of other developing nations. It is also widely held that FDI can lift millions of people out of poverty, and has a character of capacity building for physical infrastructure, on which international business relies, that in the end should be advantageous, to citizens of the world.

By thinking about a parallel global institution, such as the New Development Bank, BRICS nations are thinking of global strategies, which are running in competition with the IMF, and World Bank, for infrastructure developments, after their repeated calls for major representation. The investments can have a significant impact on services, including employment, knowledge transfer, and enhanced competition.

The diplomacy has been to promote bilateral, and multi-lateral agreements, on common themes, such as standards of treatment, as well as dispute settlement, allowances for a public interest, and ease, from barriers, for market suppliers.

 BRICS nations are also rooting for a new global currency, after several falls in the value of the US dollar, in the recent past. There is a huge scope for this new bloc, in identifying the sectors, for their pattern of investments, which has also given rise to several social issues, to be addressed, and the legal compliance, that comes with it.

These steps have proved positive, in terms of rapid economic growth, ever since the financial crises of 2008 happened, due to greater trust bondage, and rationality between the BRICS nations, through numerous global summits.

BRICS bloc has been currently devising a $100 billion fund to stabilise the currency markets.

All these strategies are an attempt to rebalance the global economy that gives plenty of scope, for an optimistic debate for prosperity.

30 September, 2015

48

PEACE CONUNDRUM OF THE UNITED STATES

AMERICAN IMPERIALISM DID NOT begin with the wars in Iraq and Afghanistan. Historians have long traced its roots to the late nineteenth century, particularly to 1898, when the United States annexed Hawaii and emerged from the Spanish-American War with control over Puerto Rico, Guam, and the Philippines. Contemporary observers recognised these developments as a significant departure from the country's earlier continental expansion, marking its emergence as an overseas power with strategic interests extending across the Caribbean and the Pacific. The acquisition of these territories laid the foundations for a global presence that would shape American foreign policy throughout the twentieth century and beyond.

This expansionist logic continued to evolve during the Cold War. Under President Ronald Reagan, the United States became deeply involved in the conflicts of Central America, supporting anti-communist governments and insurgent groups in countries such as Nicaragua, El Salvador, and Guatemala. Journalists and human rights organisations documented how American military aid, intelligence assistance, and political backing strengthened regimes and armed actors accused of widespread abuses. Critics argued that the pursuit of geopolitical objectives often came at the expense of democratic accountability and human rights, while supporters maintained that such policies were necessary to contain Soviet influence in the Western Hemisphere.

By the 1990s, debates over American power had shifted rather than disappeared. Critics increasingly argued that US foreign policy combined economic globalisation with a willingness to employ military force when strategic interests were perceived to be at stake. Interventions in the Balkans and continued engagement in the Middle East led some scholars and commentators to view American policy as an extension of post-Cold War primacy, designed to preserve a favourable international order under US leadership. Supporters, however, contended that these interventions reflected humanitarian concerns and efforts to maintain regional stability rather than imperial ambition.

The presidency of George W. Bush intensified these debates. Following the attacks of 11 September 2001, the United States launched military campaigns in Afghanistan and Iraq, expanding its security presence across the Middle East. Journalists and analysts examined the consequences of these interventions, particularly their effects on regional politics and sectarian relations. David Rose reported in Vanity Fair that Bush administration officials supported security forces associated with Fatah leader Muhammad Dahlan to counter Hamas in Gaza. Critics, including Rose, argued that this policy contributed to escalating tensions between Palestinian factions and helped create conditions that culminated in violent conflict. Other media outlets similarly reported that external involvement often deepened political divisions rather than resolving them.

Barack Obama entered office promising a different approach to foreign policy, yet his presidency revealed the complexities of disentangling the United States from long-standing commitments abroad. During Obama's presidency, the United States continued substantial military assistance to Israel, culminating in a ten-year aid package agreed in 2016. Obama also welcomed aspects of the Arab Peace Initiative and repeatedly called for renewed efforts toward a two-state solution, but critics argued that these diplomatic efforts failed to produce meaningful progress.

Obama likewise faced challenges in Afghanistan. Although his administration sought to reduce the American military presence and transfer security responsibilities to Afghan forces, US troops remained in the country beyond the deadlines initially envisioned. In 2009, his administration replaced the Bush administration's planned missile-defence architecture in Eastern Europe with the European Phased Adaptive Approach, a move presented by Washington as a defensive measure but viewed with suspicion by Moscow. These disagreements contributed to continuing tensions between the United States and Russia during a period when both sides were simultaneously pursuing arms-control negotiations.

Beyond the Middle East and Europe, America's global military posture remained largely intact. The continued reliance on facilities such as Diego Garcia underscored the enduring strategic footprint of the United States in the Indian Ocean. Supporters viewed these deployments as essential components of international security and power projection, while critics argued that they reflected a broader pattern of military entrenchment across key geopolitical regions.

Meanwhile, the Israeli-Palestinian conflict remained a central source of controversy. Monitoring organisations documented the continued expansion of Israeli settlements in the West Bank, while many analysts argued that such growth complicated prospects for a viable Palestinian state. Obama's visit to Israel and the Palestinian territories in 2008 as a presidential candidate, together with his repeated emphasis on Israel's security concerns during his presidency, reinforced perceptions among many Arabs and Palestinians that American policy remained tilted toward Israel. Although successive administrations expressed support for peace negotiations, critics frequently argued that diplomatic initiatives were not matched by sufficient pressure to alter realities on the ground.

These developments fuelled broader debates about the consequences of American power. Critics contended that military interventions, alliances with authoritarian partners, and selective applications of international norms contributed to regional instability and created conditions that militant groups could exploit. Supporters countered that many conflicts stemmed from local political dynamics, historical grievances, and ideological movements that predated or transcended American involvement. The resulting debate remains one of the central questions in contemporary international relations.

The broader narrative often described by critics as American imperialism is therefore not confined to the post-9/11 era but stretches back more than a century. From the territorial acquisitions of 1898 to Cold War interventions in Latin America, from the wars launched after 11 September to the diplomatic dilemmas of the Obama years, scholars and journalists have repeatedly examined the ways in which American power has been projected abroad. Reports from major international media organisations, academic studies, and human rights investigations have documented both the reach of US influence and the controversies surrounding its exercise.

What remains unresolved is whether these policies have produced more stability than instability. Critics argue that while they have strengthened American influence and preserved strategic advantages, they have also generated resentment, intensified sectarian tensions, and contributed to recurring cycles of violence. Others maintain that American engagement has often prevented wider conflicts, supported allies, and upheld elements of the international order. The persistence of these competing interpretations reflects the complexity of assessing a global power whose actions have shaped political realities across multiple continents.

Viewed over the long term, the continuity of American power projection appears less accidental than structural. Successive administrations have inherited extensive military commitments, economic interests, and strategic alliances, adapting them to changing circumstances rather than fundamentally abandoning them. Whether future leaders will challenge this framework or continue to operate within it remains uncertain. The question is not merely how American influence will evolve, but whether alternative approaches can emerge that balance security, stability, sovereignty, and democratic principles in regions long affected by intervention. Only time will reveal which path prevails.

15 September, 2015

49

PAST AND PRESENT OF CHILE

CHILE HAS BEEN KNOWN IN HISTORY as the world's second-largest copper mine pit. There was a time when the copper minefields at Chuquicamata, El Salvador mine, and El Teniente, became to be known as 'Chile's salary.'

The area had self-sustained settlements, rail networks, schools, stores, and even police forces.

Che Guevara's memoirs, *The Motorcycle Diaries*, present an anguish of sorts, after visiting the place, which he had read about only in books, where the mining workers were ill-treated, by their bosses.

When he and his friend, Granada visit the mining country, they meet a homeless communist couple searching for work. 'By the light of the single candle … the contracted features of the worker gave off a mysterious and tragic air … the couple, frozen stiff in the desert night, hugging one another, was a live representation of the proletariat of any part of the world,' Che wrote. These moments in Chile, ultimately shaped his political consciousness, against economic inequalities, in Latin America.

Many workers had stained this place with their blood, building it. At that time, US multinational corporate monopolies were expeditious and were viewed, by many, as imperial domination.

In 1971, when Salvador Allende won the election, as a socialist, he wanted to end the problem by complete nationalisation of Chilean major industries. He had introduced the idea of 'excessive profits,' of the worldwide profits of these corporations, going back to the invested state. The US department of state viewed it 'as a serious infraction to international practice, which could damage not only Chile but many developing countries as well.'

However, the 1973 coup of Allende's government, by the military junta, which was backed by the CIA, changed the political climate. It was mainly because the Communist party in Chile, considered Fidel Castro's way of governance, the ideal way, of ruling the state's social and economic system. The comrades in Chile, enjoy a large following, amongst its youth, even today.

Soon afterwards, the ideology was dissolved, by the Pinochet regime that adopted a free market model, financed by the CIA, and guarded by American economists, known as the Chicago Boys, because most of them had done postgraduate programs, in Chicago.

Once in government positions, they immediately made several structural reforms, price liberalisation, elimination of trade barriers, privatisation of state-owned companies, monetary expansion, and privatisation of social security.

Many tainted the primal success of Chile's economic miracle, to its Constitution of 1935, which gave restraints, in changing its economic model.

As a result, the Chilean economy improved. The country had also introduced a popular voucher program, where students could get an education at private schools, with the help of government resources, and parental assistance.

In the last thirty-five years, poverty fell from 50 per cent to 11 per cent, per capita income drastically increased, and inflation drastically decreased to 250 per cent. However, many claim that free market policies, introduced by the Pinochet regime, were far less than a miracle.

The market output had fallen by 15%, wages dropped to their one-third, and unemployment rose to 20%. The average GDP was 1.5%, which was lower than the average GDP of 4.5 %, in other Latin American countries, between 1970 to 1980. In the same period, GDP grew only by 8%, while for Latin America as a whole, it grew by 40%.

The neo-classical economics, of the Pinochet regime, made things worse, for the labour class, and domestic industry lost its way, generating more local jobs. About 113 protestors were killed, in the early 1980s. It also allowed an overhaul of the labour system, eliminating collective bargaining, and allowing massive dismissal of workers.

During Pinochet's rule, only the rich became wealthier and enjoyed liberties. Economic liberty and social justice did not exist, contrary to arguments, that were made about the country's economic miracle.
Freedom of the press was not allowed, against the privileged classes. Even the education system was not set to change, which many regard, as cruel. In Chile, the police state controlled the interests of wealthy capitalists. Only those with power, and wealth, did well with the experiment.

A political scientist would often ponder: are liberal policies better to structure institutions, or there is a dire need for social equality? Poor depend upon investments and job creation, to make their bread. These experiences, if taken note of, could help any developing country, in a healthy economic progression. But things could turn good for Chile, in the next four to five years.

The former President, Michelle Bachelet had proposed a welfare state that will provide all benefits to its people, and will replace the market, as the engine of growth.

Some proposals include the takeover of education, by the government, a dramatic increase in tax for corporations, and switching the social security system to betterment.

6 July, 2015

50

WORLD TRADE ORGANISATION ROUNDS

AN INTERESTING DEBATE RAGES IN THE global business arena. Tariffs and international policies, on trade, make up a huge chunk of economic decisions, in our world.

Today, many people criticise the trade liberalisation policies, around the world. After the end of the Second World War, the Bretton Woods assemblage of international economic institutions, paved the way, for one of the most important events in history.

International free trade alliances were given an advent, for a purpose, to stabilise the global economy. During those times, there was a natural urge, amidst several countries, to escape protectionist policies, about economies.

During the years 1948 to 1994, GATT (General Agreements on Tariffs and Trade) saw high growth turnouts in international commerce, which was later constituted as the WTO, in 1995.

Uruguay Round, from 1986 to 1994, was conducted seven times, over the years, that mainly focused on agricultural subsidies, banking, and foreign investment. The Doha Development Round was the next, constituted in 2001, having missed its deadline of completion, in 2005.

The 'Doha Development Round' is mainly aiming to reduce trade barriers, around the world.

The negotiations, however, have collapsed over special safeguard mechanisms, in agricultural trade between the United States, China and India. European Trade Commissioner, Peter Madelson called it a 'collective failure.'

He believes that the farm bills, drafted by the US Congress, were 'reactionary,' and were harmed by its five-year program, of agricultural subsidies.

UK Prime Minister, David Cameron, on the other hand, invited ridicule, over the timing of the development round, at the 2011 World Economic Forum, held in Davos.

In April 2011, the then director- general, Pascal Lamy asked members to think hard about the consequences, of 'throwing away years of solid multi-lateral work.' After that, in December 2013, director general Roberto Azevedo, presented a part of the Doha Round, focused on intellectual property issues, trade facilitation, and food security.

A recent study related to the Doha Development Round claims, that if WTO members reduce agricultural subsidies by 33%, there will be an increase of $574 billion US dollars, around the globe.

World Bank's lead economist, Kym Anderson, believes that the Doha Round deals could yield up to $2500 to $3000 billion. These monies might eventually end up in the developing world.

Copenhagen Consensus, a project that seeks to evaluate global welfare measures, using theories of welfare economies, ranked Doha Round, as the second best for global investment.

WTO, conversely, also has been increasingly gaining adversaries, over the years. It has been tainted as being inclined towards the policies of developed countries.

World Development Movement has not been in its favour, nor has the World Social Forum. Martin Khor, director of an inter-government organisation, South Centre, believes that WTO policy measures are biased towards developing nations, in terms of having access to technologies, high import duties by rich countries, and anti-dumping measures, allowed against developing countries, to name a few.

Subsidies are often paid to rich farmers. The Fair-Trade argument has not been regulated well. It is also very hard for WTO to reach a common consensus, from all its member states, thereby affecting sound decision-making. The poorest cannot get good access to medicines. The reach of its legal system is not effective, in developing nations.

The international organisation has also been criticised for adverse job effects, like job loss for justified tariffs, an entity that cuts growth in sectors, and innovations to maintain high profits, as postulated, by Noam Chomsky.

When an exported product enters a country, it has the potential to raise the prices, of domestic goods, as well. In that sense, a tariff works as a wealth transfer tax, for a noncompetitive product.

The organisation has also been criticised, for the way it handles, dispute resolutions, between member states, and for its transparency. Its critics view it as a machine, for stronger nations, to control weaker nations. John Dearden, chairman of WDM, believes that there have been so many deals going out, outside the frays of WTO, which are not pro-poor, especially deals done, by the Obama administration.

People, all over the world, want people to shift from corporations to people. These developments have not been received well, by many social movements, going on, around the world.

If we dive into history, the protests of Seattle in 1999, and to recent protests of Bali, in 2013, all point out the same root problems, which are related to bad diplomacy, and badly woven trade policies, at the international scale.

7 September, 2014

51

THE OTTOMAN REVIVAL

AFTER THE END OF THE FIRST World War, and the signing of the Treaty of Versailles in 1919, the Ottomans lost all their territories.

The Ottoman Empire was one of the most powerful Islamic Empires (1290-1918). In the 16th century, it enjoyed a peak of its power, by ruling the entire Middle East, and North Africa, under the rule of Sultan Selim I, followed by the rule of Sultan Suleyman, who overtook North Africa excluding Morocco. Known as the 'Protectors of the Pilgrimage,' they even once ruled Mecca and Medina.

History has shown that once an empire collapses, its remnants somehow, remain. We are seeing Putin trying to sell Russian national ideas, in places such as Crimea. A similar debate, happening in Ankara, is no exception to this rule.

Throughout the epochs of history, we have heard good of Ottoman commerce, laws, and several aspects of their civil administration, that existed, in the 20th century.

Ottomans were known to create a power structure, designed to overcome challenges, in governance, because the empire covered vast geographical spheres, covering an entire spectrum of social organisations, from urban cities to rural populations. Nomadic pastoralist communities, like Berbers, Bedouins, and Turkmen, still exist, as races, to date.

Many missionaries, dervishes, pilgrims, and traders brought with them their language, religion, and culture, and contributed vastly to the Ottoman empire such as Druzes, Christians, Slavic languages, and Russian dialects, to name a few.

No one can also deny the deserving survival of Ottoman architecture, and its influence on music, cuisine, Arab language, and heritage, among others, till today.

The reign of Sultan Abdul Hamid II, in Ottoman Palestine, is well recorded, apart from other role models. 'Ottoman Empire has left an imprint on history, which was backed by modernization, and self-confidence,' Albert Hourani wrote, in his research notes.

Having said that, few modern Middle East observers, of history, have commented, on the bad side of Ottoman history.

The grotesque of the Ottoman army has not been articulated well, in media machines, where all male subjects of the empire, between 17- 55, were forcefully recruited, into the army.

The Sultan often pampered the officer class, while the foot soldiers were often left underprivileged. Rich young boys often used to give bribes, to manage their way out, of public service, and some were eventually sent to combat, in far-off places.

The tales of the struggles of a Lebanese village, to smuggle wheat, in the dreaded war of *Safar Barlik*, were often recorded, and narrated, by an elite few.

Many commoners used to be punished on the battlefront. Over 2.8 million were sent to war, and 325,000 died between 1914 and 1918.

This anguish of war, was destructive, to both rich and poor, in Ottoman Syria, where many families shivered, in the winter of 1915.

More agony, followed in the same year, when famine broke out, in the Port of Beirut, where many flocked into Damascus, and died of hunger.

The population there dropped, from 180,000 to 75,000, from 1914 to 1916. 'People were dying on the streets every day,' Sami Moubayed said, a Syrian historian, and a Carnegie scholar.

Ottomans, between 1914-1924 were responsible for the Assyrian genocide, called Seyfo, often carried out by Kurdish tribes. The Armenian Genocide, committed between 1915-1917, resulted in over 1.5 million deaths, during the government of the Committee of Union and Progress.

Turkish leaders, like Prime Minister Erdogan, know about their mournful history. He, therefore, wants to promote the good side of the Ottoman era and is thus working for its revival.

Although being in an alliance, with the British, against the Arabs, by selling Ottoman Palestine, to the Zionists, in the Great War, Turkey today wants a brotherly expansion, of the Ottoman culture, in the Arab region.

His approach has worked well to some extent, by engaging

with the political actors in opposition in Damascus, who now talk about the good side of Ottoman - Arab history, as well.

The recent Ottoman traditions looked at French-oriented culture, in Europe, for inspiration and alliances.

The AK Party, in Turkey, takes pride in its centre - right position, in Turkish politics. It is an approach that resonates well, largely, in average Anatolian populations. The country also wants a similar British Commonwealth role, in the Arab region.

However, the present ruling AK party views Turkey, as part of the western coalition, but is also posing a clear departure from the late Ottoman period. It may reflect a warning sign.
These political stances are part of the neo-Ottomanism strategy, implemented by Turkey internationally, which are mostly economic, and political, in nature.

In Ankara's political chambers, the debate rages to balance the historic Ottoman view of governance, to the current scenario. Their actions are getting implemented, because of the consciousness, and interpretations, of their history.

Importantly, there was an urgent realisation of the fact that the geo-political position, of Turkey, in the world, should prove beneficial regionally, but also with a prudent global strategy.

However, more recently, the formation of 'Free Syrian Army' and Turkish backed 'Syrian National Council,' has breached the UN Charter, and have attacked Syrian sovereignty, with the help of Turkish intelligence, that have again raised questions, regarding peace and development, in the region.

The rise of Qatari - Turkish-backed FSA has also faded to *Salafi*-backed organisations in Syria, especially ISIS which wants an Islamic State in Iraq. So, what is in store in terms of Ottoman revival? More war and less peace, to be precise.

1 July, 2014

52

KAZAKHSTAN'S ALLIANCE WITH EURO ASIAN ECONOMIC UNION

THE BIRTH OF EURO ASIAN ECONOMIC UNION IS Vladimir Putin's brainchild and Russia's answer to the European Union (EU).

Putin dreams of creating a tariff-free trade zone, along with other member states, thereby fostering closer socio-economic ties.

All this strategical exercise must go well, with the other two players, namely Kazakhstan and Belarus. More importantly, Russia must bring the political actors, in Astana, closer to its Moscow plan, because Kazakhstan, has pivotal stakes, in the region.

Russia, and Kazakhstan, share common pipelines, an electricity grid, and railway links, which cover 4000 miles of the border. Astana will have the region's tallest skyscraper, very soon.

In terms of bilateral achievements, Russia did business with over \$26 billion, in 2013, alone. Russia is also a main consumer, of Kazakhstan, in mining and chemical exports.

World's largest spaceport, Baikonur Cosmodrome, is managed by Russia, in Kazakhstan. About 50 per cent of Kazakhs speak Russian, and 85 can read, and write in Russian, signifying similar cultural ties.

Putin still emphasises a softer approach, in terms of having ties with Kazakhstan, where Russia influences media control, and funding many pro-Russian institutions, in culture and language.

Having said this, all is not going well with the Kazakh state actors. Its president, Nazarbayev wants a limit, Russian sponsored channels, in Cosmodrome, with more Kazakh language, in the Internet content.

In 2012, Nazarbayev announced, that the country would switch from Cyrillic letters to Roman alphabets, a move, which signifies strong regionalism in politics, and a stance, which is allowing them to move away, from Russian dominance.

In terms of war mongering, by Russia, when it announced to attack the Crimean Peninsula, by launching a coup d'état, against its President Viktor Yanukovych, Kazakhstan's government openly espoused 'independence' for Ukraine.

To add more fuel to the fire, an anti-EEU protest, held in Almaty, attended by 500 people, signified that all is not well, in their international diplomacy.

Putin, who once aspired, to move its member states, towards greater political, economic, and military stability, is losing ground, in terms of sustainable leadership.

Kazakhstan has also rejected the common currency, collective parliament, and common passport, among others, with Russia. Many political analysts are hinting, that the future political moves, by Russia, towards Kazakhstan, maybe aggressive, nonetheless.

In terms of its domestic strategy, Kazakhstan is trying to

implement harsher criminal codes, on separatist activities, by increasing prison sentences.

The government is also trying to shift hundreds, of ethnic Kazakhs, to the Russian-speaking regions. Several activists, like Maria Chichtchenkova, hint at a further downfall, in the Russian institutions, in the country.

The country is also concerned about Kazakh citizens, of the northern region, who have been successful, in gaining Russian passports, and about the control of Moscow, in regional media machines.

Kazakhstan has been a flashpoint in 'The New Great Game,' between China, and Russia, in terms of energy supply. Some political analysts, like Cooley, suggest, that its growing relationship with China, may leverage the country, towards imposing Russian influences.

China has been investing in the country's pipelines, helping to pay for the country's energy infrastructure, and providing emergency loans, for Kazakh-run state businesses.

In 2013 alone, Chinese President Xi Jingping struck $30 billion deals with Kazakhstan's government, including a $5 billion deal, for a Chinese oil corporation, to build an offshore project, in the country.

China is already connected to Kazakh oil, via a 1400-mile pipeline, which bought up at least 40 per cent of Kazakhstan's hydrocarbon assets, recalls Georgi Kantchev, a free-lance journalist, based in London.

Now Kazakhstan is geo-politically strangled, between new Chinese engagements, and old ties with Russia.

However, last month only, at the meeting of the Assembly of Kazakhstan, the leader proclaimed, having good relations, with both countries.

For how long, can we expect to see stability and optimism, from Russia's political moves, towards its EEU member state?

The two-fold approach, as a political manoeuvre, does not work, for long. Maybe, Kazakhstan must choose its sole ally, between the two neighbours, very quickly.

19 June, 2014

53

SUFFERING OF PALESTINIANS THAT NEVER ENDED

WHEN A NEW NATIONALIST MOVEMENT WAS BORN, in Europe, advocating the creation of a Jewish state, in the First Zionist Congress of 1897, its delivery resulted in about exodus of 750,000 Palestinians, who were made refugees, in the *Nakba* of 1948, from Palestine, which was the part of Ottoman Empire. The result was the enmity, between native Palestinian Muslims, and immigrating Jews, from Europe.

The concept of being away from their land, still emphasises their right to return, the most basic humanitarian law. It has been on the list of many leaders, most recently, in John Kerry's framework of peace, who wanted quiet diplomacy, in the Arab region.

Politically, the Oslo Accords of 1993, and the Taif Agreement of 1989, were jolted, by the *intifada*, of the common people.

In 1940, the British ended the mandate of Palestine, and left the country, on 14th May 1948. The ruling Jewish leader, Yitzhak Rabin, at that time, had signed an order, expelling Palestinians, from two towns of Lyyda and Ramala.

By the end of 1949, in *'Deir Yassin' massacre*, the war expelled 700,000 to 750,000. Only 150,000 remained in

Israel. Over 150 towns were destroyed. Many were even forcibly expelled, by Israeli forces.

The 1954, 'Prevention of Infiltration Law' allowed the Israeli government, to expel any Palestinian.

The 'Battle of Karameh,' in 1968, however, resulted in a propaganda victory of Palestinians, over Israelis, which establishes the cause of Palestinian nationhood. It gave Yasser Arafat's *Fatah* international attention, and propelled the cause, to an international scale.

King Hussein of Jordan, was so emotionally aroused, by the Palestinian victory, that he branded all of them, as 'martyrs'.

In the context of the Arab-Israeli conflict, many Arab countries, like Jordan, helped these refugees, with temporary settlements, which has ultimately made them permanently homeless.

There are also nearly half a million Palestinians, living in refugee camps, in Syria: entire refugee camps were established, about 65 years ago. The people in them were either killed or fled safely, elsewhere.

Many fight cold and shiver in snow, without a dwelling. In many of these camps, the refugees, who were kept under military seizure, literally got starved to death.

Most recently, an investigative book *'Refugees of the Revolution'* (2013), by author Diana Allan, ascertained the plight of a Palestinian living in exile, where she argued about the common assumption of their identity, from their credit associations, debt relations, immigration networks, electricity bartering, and NGO planning.

In many parts of Palestine, what is now Israel, everyone, is more, or less, a refugee. When PLO's provocation invoked a civil war, from 1975 to 1990, including a horrendous *'War of the Camps,'* between 1985 to 1988, it did not integrate them with the Lebanese, and even now, the Israeli military is creating more Palestinian refugees, who are being thrown out, of their ancestral homes.

In West Bank, people's homes are demolished almost every week, for a while. Palestinians, ironically, are a bunch of people, who do not hold any citizenship, or any right of return.

The influential, and the rich segment of the population, have migrated, to better countries, due to a sense of isolation, and neglect.

Palestinian refugees, however, are getting regrouped, near Handarat camp in Aleppo, Syria, to a 3,000,000-strong community in Chile, Lebanon, occupied Jerusalem, France, Australia, United Kingdom, to Balata camp in Nablus, Deraa camp in Syria, and Al Amari camp, in Ramallah.

To initiate some sort of political courage, today, many Palestinians are raising the flag of return, under the banner 'Return Unifies Us,' through an amalgam of civil coalitions, from the besieged Yarmouk camp of Damascus. The Yarmouk youth band hold concerts, in candlelight, near the Turkish border.

Posters, exhibitions, lectures, rallies, and marching scouts, define Palestinian unity, and their sense of humanity and dignity.

They have the power to fashion their fate, and this

has rejuvenated the cause of their liberation, and return.

16 June, 2016

54

MILITARY RED TAPE IN AFRICA

THE SLOGAN THAT AFRICA IS RISING has been lingering around, for a while now, with many multinationals, wanting to invest, in the continent. It is because Africa, today, is marketed, by many business leaders of the West, as the next generation economy.

However, these slogans, have been tired of late, because of the increasing social ills, eating into the system, which is directly affecting nearly 1.1 billion inhabitants.

In September 2013, about sixty-seven people, died in Kenya, in a Westgate Mall siege, where the country showed to the world, that it was unable to police itself.

In Nigeria, about 200 school children were abducted, by Boko Haram, in a series of calculating attacks, where its army took the toll of failing, for their freedom.

The armies of Africa are regarded as one of the best assets, in these countries.

Such is their pride and confidence, that in the year 1994, when the Rwandan genocide happened, Africans were bold enough to recognise their security, by gradually phasing out of the alliance, on armed interventions, from the West. Countries, like Nigeria and Kenya, proved pivotal, in such an effort.

Nigeria, which has recently taken over South Africa, as the biggest economy in Africa, has provided the regional muscle for the Economic Community of West African States (ECOWAS), serving both Liberia and Sierra Leone.

Its Joint Task Force (JTF) has contributed to peacekeeping operations, in the former Yugoslavia and East Timor, and has even dispatched soldiers to Somalia, Darfur, the Democratic Republic of Congo, and Mali.

The Kenyan Defence Forces, which was widely acclaimed, for keeping the 2007 presidential election, in a favourable light, are viewed in the West as important instruments, against the Al Shabaab infiltration.
The KDF has more than 3000 men, deployed in southern Somalia. Having said this, many questions have been raised, about their operational reliability.

When Islamic extremists attacked the Westgate shopping mall in September 2013, KDF (Kenyan Defence Forces), shot the elite counter-intelligence units, who had secured the premises which were followed by extensive frisking, and investigation, in the area.

A fortnight later, Nigerian parents, whose children were abducted by some Boko Haram militants, were so infuriated by the local army, that they set out to the jungle hideouts of these militias in the hope of finding their kids.

The social media campaigns, against these instances, have turned more vocal than ever, and there are even reports, where the military fails to launch successful operations, against Boko Haram.

African States, in general, have not shared intimate

relations with the army powers. Facts reveal that it has been the Nigerian army, of the 1990s, that was involved in diamond smuggling, and drug trafficking.

The green men, in uniform, that symbolise law and order, have been victimised by various opportunistic factions in the society. The institutions, it has constructed, are rudimentary and fragile, due to weak civilian governments.

Presidents like Zaire Mobutu Sese Seko, has himself staged two successful coups, and deliberately kept national armies, divided and faction-ridden. Zimbabwe's generals became deeply involved in the Democratic Republic of Congo's diamond and gold mining.

When we talk of Nigeria, the military coups stretch back, to 1966, after the country gained independence, from Britain. It only ended in 1999, with the election of President Olusegun Obasanjo. He retired more than 400 army officers, who seemingly were more interested in politics, than the military. Uganda's generals, also, have been accused, of unnecessarily prolonging the war, on the Lord's Resistance Army, in the north of their country.

Today, the debate rages, about whether the army faces logistical challenges, to rescue the abducted school girls, from these forests, which are twice in size as Belgium, as narrated by authors, like Michela Wrong, who has published books, on the politics that has plagued countries, like Kenya, Eritrea, and Republic of Congo.

The debate has even extended to topics, such as Boko Haram having good knowledge of military movements, and budgetary failures, where living conditions of army, unpaid wages, and weaker equipment, have contributed to pitiful army operations.

Police in Kenya have been a product of systematic sleaze, where bribery is extracted, routinely.

One of the characteristics that led to the Westgate attack was the absence of any prior intelligence, about the imminent attack, the country's immigration posts, and police stations were functionally, useless.

For this reason, many strategists have argued that traditional training must go, and skills in dealing in these sensitive situations, should come from abroad, like 'anti-terrorist experts,' from France.

15 June, 2014

55

ARABS SUPPORT MILITARY RULERS

THREE MILITARY FIGURES HAVE EMERGED as significant actors in the politics of Libya, Egypt, and Lebanon. In Libya, Field Marshal Khalifa Haftar commands the self-styled Libyan National Army and has positioned himself as one of the most influential figures in shaping the country's future. Reporting by Reuters and The Guardian has documented how Haftar's campaigns in Benghazi and Tripoli received support from foreign powers, including Russia and the United Arab Emirates, while his reliance on foreign fighters and mercenaries has drawn criticism from international organisations and human rights groups. Critics argue that his military dominance has weakened prospects for democratic governance, even as supporters portray him as a force for stability and order.

In Egypt, Abdel Fattah al-Sisi rose from general to president following the military's removal of Mohamed Morsi in 2013. Since assuming office, Sisi has consolidated power through the military establishment while presenting himself as a guarantor of stability amid regional turmoil. Reuters, Amnesty International, and other observers have documented restrictions on civil society, arrests of activists, limitations on political opposition, and tighter control over public discourse. Supporters credit his government with maintaining security and pursuing large infrastructure projects, while critics argue that political freedoms have been significantly curtailed.

Lebanon's former army commander Jean Qahwaji was periodically discussed as a potential presidential candidate, though his political influence never approached the level exercised by either Haftar or Sisi. His name nevertheless surfaced in debates about military influence in Lebanese politics. L'Orient Today reported that investigations into alleged illicit enrichment involving Qahwaji and other former security officials were ultimately affected by statutes of limitation, a development that reflected broader concerns about accountability within Lebanon's political and judicial systems.

The wider Arab region has long been shaped by military intervention in politics. Egypt's modern era of military rule began with the 1952 Free Officers coup that brought Gamal Abdel Nasser and his colleagues to power. In Libya, Muammar Gaddafi overthrew King Idris in 1969 and established a system that concentrated authority in the hands of the state and security apparatus. In Yemen, Ali Abdullah Saleh maintained power through a complex web of tribal alliances and patronage networks. Similarly, Houari Boumedienne in Algeria and Hafez al-Assad in Syria consolidated highly centralised political systems that restricted opposition and strengthened military influence over public life. These histories illustrate how military institutions have repeatedly shaped governance across the region, often limiting the development of democratic institutions.

Recent developments demonstrate that military rulers continue to be viewed by some segments of society as figures capable of imposing order during periods of instability. Yet the persistence of armed extremist organisations and unresolved political grievances means that stability remains fragile. In Egypt, the Muslim Brotherhood strongly opposed the military's removal of

Morsi and continues to regard the event as a coup. Electoral participation has varied over time, reflecting a mixture of support, apathy, and political disillusionment. In Libya, Haftar has consistently portrayed himself as an opponent of political Islam and has promoted reconstruction and development projects in eastern Libya, although critics argue that military dominance continues to overshadow meaningful political reform.

Religious minorities often find themselves caught between competing political forces. In some countries, segments of Christian communities have viewed secular military rulers as a lesser threat than extremist Islamist movements that have targeted minority populations. However, such attitudes vary widely across societies and should not be treated as uniform. The rise of extremist organisations such as ISIS created profound insecurity for Christians, Yazidis, and other minority groups across Iraq and Syria, reinforcing fears about sectarian violence and political instability.

At the same time, accountability and reform remain pressing concerns throughout the region. Economic hardship, unemployment, corruption, and weak institutions continue to fuel public frustration. Human Rights Watch, Amnesty International, and numerous international observers have repeatedly documented how authoritarian governments often suppress dissent while struggling to deliver durable political and economic reforms. Critics argue that long-term stability requires stronger institutions, greater transparency, and wider political participation rather than reliance on coercive state power alone.

The identification of dissenters remains a sensitive issue. Liberal reformers, civil society activists, journalists, and opposition figures have frequently challenged emergency laws and the expanding role of military institutions in civilian governance. Their resistance reflects a broader tension between authoritarian rule and demands for political freedom. Many of the uprisings associated with the Arab Spring were driven by frustration with corruption, repression, economic inequality, and the absence of meaningful democratic participation. Subsequent crackdowns resulted in arrests, imprisonment, and restrictions on political activity, drawing sustained criticism from international human rights organisations and global media outlets.

Authoritarianism has remained a dominant feature of governance across much of the Arab world for decades. The central question is whether military-led governments can provide lasting stability and economic development while also addressing demands for political inclusion and accountability. Some citizens view strong leadership and order as necessary responses to instability, while others contend that democratic institutions, however imperfect, remain essential for sustainable progress. Stability may generate optimism, but the balance between security and freedom remains one of the defining political challenges facing the region.

Extending this analysis, one sees how military figures continue to embody both promise and peril. Haftar's dependence on foreign support highlights the continuing fragility of Libyan sovereignty and state institutions. Sisi's consolidation of power illustrates how military leaders can entrench themselves politically while limiting independent civic space. Qahwaji's comparatively limited role in Lebanon demonstrates the constraints imposed by that country's sectarian political system, where military figures may wield influence but rarely dominate national politics outright.

The press has played a crucial role in documenting these developments. Reuters and The Guardian have reported extensively on Haftar's foreign backing and military campaigns. Reuters, Amnesty International, BBC reporting, and other observers have scrutinised Egypt's restrictions on dissent and political opposition. L'Orient Today has highlighted accountability challenges within Lebanon's political and security institutions. Human rights organisations have consistently warned about the dangers of unchecked military power, while international publications have documented the human consequences of repression and political conflict.

Ultimately, the persistence of military influence in the Arab world raises profound questions about the relationship between stability, security, and democratic governance. While some communities welcome the order imposed by powerful military institutions, others fear the erosion of civil liberties and the perpetuation of authoritarian rule. The region's future will depend on whether reformers, political leaders, and civil society organisations can strengthen accountability and representative institutions, or whether military dominance will continue to define political life. The historical record suggests that stability achieved through coercion alone is rarely permanent, making the search for accountable governance one of the most important challenges facing the contemporary Arab world.

31 May, 2014

56

THE TRUE SOCIALIST IN HUGO CHAVEZ

HUGO CHAVEZ DIED ON CANCER on 5 March, 2013. His body has been embalmed, and put on display, in a glass casket for eternity, at a military museum, after a big state funeral, like the one, which has not been seen, since the death of Argentina's Eva Peron, before the country braces itself, for a tumultuous election campaign.

This Latin American Socialist icon had been widely regarded as one of its most popular leaders, amongst the new wave of leftist parties, that are working for the emancipation of Latin American countries.

Chavez was seen as a virile force of nationalisation, by the Venezuelans. In this political career, he drew inspiration from the Cuban Revolution, the leftist governments of Juan Alvarado, and Omar Torrijos, in Panama.

He used his country's rich natural reserves, such as oil, for the poor, for which he was seen as their liberator. He invested millions of dollars, in oil, in countries, that were ideologically similar.

In 1992, Chavez launched Revolutionary Bolivarian Movement, against President Carlos Andres Perez. After the death of 18 lives and 60 injuries, he gave himself up, and languished in prison, for two years, when his associates tried to seize power, but they failed again.

As a leader for Venezuelans, he spoke, wrote, and read widely. He delivered forty hours of speeches per week. He discussed his policies frequently, on radio and television.

Alo Presidente (Hello President), the programme where his policies were discussed, had no time limits. Chavez preferred weekly meetings, with his cabinet, to stay in direct contact, with the masses.

Born in the small village of Sabaneta, in July 1954, and popularly known as *'Commandante,'* Chavez was a proponent of Bolivarian Nationalism.

Chavez started his journey, as a small-time schoolteacher, where he educated army officers, with heroic tales of Simon Bolivar, that called an end to Spanish colonialism. Bolivar was a freedom fighter, who won independence from many countries, in the early 1800s.

He tried to embody himself as the next Che. His early start in politics defined grass root level democracy.

Chavez even tried his best to decentralise. In 1999, he passed a referendum, regarding whether, or not, Venezuela wanted a constituent assembly, a second assembly, or a second referendum, ratifying the new constitution.

The most considerate welfare measure, that Chavez took that year, was introducing articles, that gave freedom to mixed races and black people.

The little *'Red Book'* of the Venezuelan Constitution became a best seller, for the people, on the streets. 'The indigenous peoples, it says, have the right to maintain their economic practices, based on reciprocity, solidarity and exchange and to define their priorities.'

Its popularity, was such, that articles of the book, were even written on the soap power packets, found in commercial retail chains.

Chavez's social missions provided free healthcare, and education, at the university level, to formerly excluded people, which eventually changed their life, and outlooks.

He began real land reforms and guaranteed women's rights. The facts speak for themselves: the percentage of people in poverty fell from 55%, in 1995, to 26.4%, in 2009. When Chavez was sworn into office, unemployment was 15%.

In June 2009, it was 7.8%. The poorest housewives got at least 120 pounds a month.

Chavez won eight elections, and eight referendums in eight years, which is regarded as a world record.

'The 2002 Venezuelan coup' attempt, ousted him for 47 hours, but he was luckily restored, by a combination of military loyalists, and massive public support, for his government.

It was a failed attempt by Pedro Carmona, who headed an amalgam of pro-business elites, known as the Venezuelan Federation of Chambers and Commerce (FEDECAMARAS).

'On August 1805,' wrote Chavez, Bolívar 'climbed the Monte Sacro near Rome and made a solemn oath.' Like Bolívar, Chavez swore to break the chains binding Latin Americans to the will of the mighty. He owed much of his education to avowed Marxist, Salvador Allende, the Socialist leader of Chile.

He wanted to be a pacifist and a democrat like him. Chavez drew lessons, from the coup of Allende in Chile, and it shaped his belief system, against far-right democracies, and cruel imperialist policies, that served as ordeals for the poor countries.

Chavez even had his critics. To many local media outlets, he was seen as a repressor, as he clamped down on their services. His social programs were criticised because they soared up inflation and decreased production. To businessmen, he was seen as a proponent, who was an antagonist to investments. His legacy, in the world, today, has received mixed reactions.

His governance had proved as a threat, to the United States' policies, for their local alliances with the elite anti-left, especially the wealthy business class, in Caracas, who owned villas in Miami. Interestingly, his dictatorship was not seen as authoritarianism by the people. It is because he constantly challenged actions against cruel and oligarchical servants, and for this reason, his populism won support from the common masses.

In 2009, his rule announced unlimited terms for his officials, and himself, a pure dictatorship for the people of Venezuela, until his sudden death.

His last words were, 'I don't want to die,' before succumbing to a massive heart attack, as narrated by his loyalist generals.

8 March, 2013

57

GRADUAL RISE OF HINDUTVA IN INDIA

INDIA AND PAKISTAN WERE FORMED through a tryst of destiny. The so-called revolutionaries rose to find the soul of their nations, which were long suppressed, according to their free thinking.

Soldiers, adventurers, businessmen, and administrators were the proudest possessions, to exploit this part of the continent, which was getting free, from the Empire of the Colonial British. They left but kept their senates, their language, and their institutions, in their respective vassals.

British ruled from Khyber Pass to Cape Camorin. Through the quarter of the century, of inspired agitations and protests, the nationalist movement grew to an unusual prominence, which made the British leave India.

The roots of this uprising were an age-old antagonism, between India's Hindus and Muslims, sustained by a tradition of antipathetic religious differences, and economic inequality, subtly exacerbated, by Britain's divide-and-rule Policy.

Thus, there was a birth of ideologies and leaders, born out of the revolting masses, which freed themselves from the British, to chalk out a future, of the sub-continent.

Muslims demanded, if an Islamic State was not formed, it would result in the bloodiest pogrom in Asian history, due to exaggerated violence.

The reason for that was the emerging force of 'Hindu Mahasabha,' the Great Hindu Society, an ideology that had a strong Hindu nationalist socio-politico overtone, with no space for Islamic reformists, or even secularists, in the emerging homeland.

Even for the Congress Party, who were representing millions of majority Hindus, at that time, the rise of the Islamist State was the mutilation of their homeland, almost sacrilegious, to which they eventually conceived.

It seemed in history that Britain was trapped between two irreconcilable positions, sinking slowly into the quagmire, from which the British Empire in India, was unable to extricate itself.

Hindu Mahasabha's central core was a society called the Hindu Rashtra Dal, which Savarkar, the movement's dictator, founded in Pune, on 15 May, 1942. They shared that leadership should be derived from the most restrictive and meaningful Indian bonds, known as caste. It had guardianship of elite Brahmins, the heirs of Peshwas.

The Brahmins, in Hindu mythology, descended from Seven Penitents, whose spirits were transformed, into social and priestly elite, and were believed to be born twice, like birds. Hinduism, as a religion, represented 'anarchic Hindu-ness.' It was a cultural and a religious phenomenon, while 'Hinduvta' was politicised faith, a kind of calculated hegemony, propagated through elite Hindu circles, guarding politics for their respective subjects, even though the movement claims to remove the vices, of social inequality, in the current times.

Hindutva also amalgamated other religions, such as Sikhism, Buddhism, and Jainism, but was generally biased towards Muslims, and Christians, and had called for a reverse in political strategy, due to their historic cultural influence, in India, which they essentially regarded, as a holy land of Hindus.

To Muslims, it is generally accepted that integrating into a 'Hindutva society' is to compromise the Muslim identity, and the theology of the Koran, which taught monotheism, like other Abrahamic religions, when competing faith-based politics, is ruling the minority.

'Hindutva' is a religious movement in the polity. It has three identifiers: 'religious, cultural and geographical'. For Hindus, religion is derived from polytheism. Islam is largely against this phenomenon. To Muhammad Ali Jinnah, the two-nation theory was expounded for the reason, that the two religious communities belonged to two different philosophies, with different social customs and literature, having no intermarriage, between various concepts, emerging through a civilisational evolution.

Even for Allama Iqbal, guardianship and emancipation of 80 million minority Muslims, before the partition era, in a majority 'Hinduised' society, was prone to dangers of extremism, and militarism, towards civil wars.

Savarkar once summarised: 'The State will not guarantee secured Muslim seats, in the Legislature, or in the Administration and, if such guarantee is insisted upon by the Muslims, such guaranteed quota is not to exceed their proportion to the general population.' Constitutionally, India recognises Muslims as equal citizens. It seems to be a legal argument that seems to be a winning reminder of Hindutva ideologues.

Jinnah, on the other hand, negated any form of faith-based

nationalism, and propagated equal treatment of non-Muslims, in Pakistani society. So, was this civilisational conflict, the birth of Pakistan as a nation, unavoidable to attain peace in South Asia?

To what extent, Hinduvta proved pivotal towards the propagation of two nation theory, and how will Sarvarkar's 'Ahkand Bharat' (United India, Pakistan, and Bangladesh) be a reality, when a country, with advantageous 'Hinduised' socio-politico dictatorship, ordains over a harmonious and a collective society in South Asia?

At the same time, Sarvarkar propagated a separate homeland for Jews in Israel, so why didn't he have the same perceptions of a separate Muslim homeland? Academics and politicians should answer the growing communal indecencies, in Indian politics, because when we look at the condition of Muslims in India, they work in apathy, and live in uncared ghettos. Ignorance and lack of secular education is also a problem for Muslims, in both nations, but communal wars between these two communities, in the past, serve as a dangerous predicament, for an ever-growing tussle, between the tenets of a Hindu Rasthra, and an Islamic State, a deepening divide, between majority and minority communities.

So, why is it a shame when Indian Muslims cannot integrate fully into the fascist-leaning, cultural Indian-ness, of a Hindutva society?

Secularism should be an answer, it should be strengthened, but it has not fully been attained in a huge country, like India, or even in Pakistan, due to dangers of religious indifferences, civilisational argumentations and extremism, which is still prevalent today, as it was during the pre-1947 era.

There needs to be liberality, economic prosperity, freedom of expression, tolerance, justice, peace, and interdependence through depoliticising faith.

However, it is a utopian dream, until people of respective religious communities, in this huge region, do not make an ideological shift, so that the place releases itself from the shackles of communal destitute, and extreme nationalism, the main forces against seeking a pluralistic union of South Asia.

22 January, 2013

58

WHEN PLANES SLAMMED THE WORLD TRADE CENTRE

We ARE APPROACHING THE TENTH anniversary, of one of the most horrific tragedies in recent memory, which shocked people the world over, killing more than a thousand of Americans. It shattered their kith and kin.

It rechristened a culture of violence. No one had ever imagined sophisticated aircrafts, serving as giant missiles, that could pass through two symbols of American financial power – World Trade Centre of New York.

The United States had never witnessed barbarity, at such a sheer scale. Much has changed ever since. Afghanistan and Iraq were invaded, and now it has paved the way for the radicalisation of its citizenries, which has provoked anger, across the Muslim world, and caused more terror attacks, in western countries.
The world also saw the end of Osama Bin Laden. He was finally killed unarmed, in an isolated compound, and dumped into international waters, by US Navy Seals in 'Operation Geromino.'

His unseen corpse was American vengeance, which caused uproar in Muslim nations, as demands for his free trial were silenced, even before anyone could think of it.

Who has been defeated? Who has attained glory, in this

clash of civilisations? Is it modern, or is it conservative? This ever-widening gap is a war, between the two worlds, which gained momentum, when several Islamic movements, decided on extremism, to oust away western influences, and activities, in their nation-states.

Clerics had viewed western cultural influences, as a mockery, of faith, Islamic theology, and its political system. War activism had gained prominence. Radicalisation grew. At a point in time, video footings, firebrand audio speeches, and radical mosque debates had started to get disseminated, all over the Middle East.

It gave reasons for the evolution of a brute civilisational war. Organisations like al-Qaeda had spearheaded this cause, against western supremacy. It all started when Bin Laden formed al-Qaeda in Afghanistan, to subdue Soviet invasion, aided by American artillery.

Upon its success, he then formed training camps, in Sudan, to expand his business operations, and began his quest, for a nuclear arsenal, which he never found. Gradually, his animosity toward growing Western influence, in Arab territories, grew, and he then glorified himself as an enemy of the United States.

From here, he was believed to have architected several attacks, on western forces, which included bombings of US embassies in Tanzania, and Kenya, aid to Somalian militias, to gun down two US Black Hawk Helicopters, followed by an attack on a US warship in Yemen, Casablanca suicide attacks, and Saudi bombings.

9/11 was the most celebrated attack by extremists. In all these cases, the hand of al-Qaeda was suspected. It became an inspirational institution for growing extremist organisations.

Although Bin Laden was killed, he not only succeeded in galvanising violence, but he also won a cardinal success against the US, by bankrupting them.

The number of military disbursals, towards wars in Iraq, and Afghanistan, crippled the American economy, at a speculative time, when the pawns of avaricious corporate influence loomed financial operations.

The massive assault, on oil-rich Muslim countries, was a merciless political plunder, and not an example of restoring the justice, and integrity of any state. By air raiding and shooting innocent victims, no one could annihilate terrorism.

It glorified United States state extremism rather. On the contrary, these immoral acts gravely outnumbered all innocent causalities, which happened on American soil.

History bears witness that America has tried to overthrow fifty-three governments, throughout its history.

The first 9/11 was carried out by Americans, in 1973, during the Nixon regime, when the United States succeeded in staging a successful coup, in overthrowing the democratically elected government of Salvador Allende, in Chile.

The United States, without a doubt, has done military aggression, in almost every Latin American country, and supported hideous regimes in countries like Turkey, Israel, West Papua and East Timor. Iraq and Afghanistan are only recent tallies.

The policies of vicious invasions by the United States are not new to this world. These illegal wars are rather a product of their gradual intolerance against humanity.

The second 9/11, a condemnable act of vengeance, came twenty-eight years later when the United States was oppressed and not the oppressor. It gave a reminder to this superpower, for its inflated pride, in neo-imperial futility.

9/11 was an angry answer from radical outfits, who believed 'USA influence' in their lands was an attack on Islam.'

This grave tragedy has also invoked a debate, on whether the institutions, or individuals, other than the perpetrators had any knowledge about the occurrence, and whether they could have made any substantive actions to prevent them.

Some theories and facts have appeared, including details about a classified military intelligence program, known as 'Able Danger,' which was created in October 1999, to target al Qaeda, where Lt. Col. Anthony Shaffer, and Congressman, Curt Weldon charged before the Senate Judiciary Committee that 'Able Danger' had identified Mohammad Atta, and three of the other hijackers, before attacks.

The 9/11 Commission had also compiled reports that suggested that Islamic extremists had given plentiful warnings, to the US about the attacks. Director of Central Intelligence, George Tenet had cautioned the administration about 'something very, very, very big.'

The Times also revealed some insider trading activity by stating several insurance companies, and airlines, who had sold off their shares, before the attack, in many countries, including the US.

It was also believed that Iranian intelligence had some information about al-Qaeda rebels taking routes, via their country.

We should increase the zeal for justice, no matter who does it, no matter who says it. If justice prevails, that is the biggest triumph. These major acts of violence have changed the world and destroyed nations.

We should put a firm faith, in our belief system, in stating that if any act of violence targeting innocent civilians is done, it should be condemned, and the people associated with it, should be brought to the book.

We should commiserate this day as a fruitful retrospection, for attaining moral elevation, to free our world from conflicts, tyranny, and subjugation.

11 September, 2011

59

BAUXITE IN THE HILLS OF ODISHA

INDIA HAS COLONISED ITSELF. The richer are getting rich in India, and the poor are getting poorer.

However, the most concerning ill, lately, has been the corporate mafia eating the system. This problem, therefore, has been met with blatant opposition from the Maoists, in the form of guerrilla rebellions.

The issue has eventually turned into the most important concern, for the ruling government in India, especially for the UPA.

Maoists, an extreme amalgam, banned by the CPI, are rebelling through the deep and isolated jungles of India, united for a cause, to oust away corporate fascism, unleashed by the Indian State, or by an amalgam of corporate elites.

In a 2009 parliamentary speech, P Chidambaram, who was himself a former committee member of the Vedanta Industry Group, openly espoused hostility, towards Left-wing extremism.

In hills of Odisha like Damanjodi and Niyamgiri, nature is God and factories are demons. The people there believe that if ecology is disturbed, their gods are sold.

It is believed Dongria Kondh people lived in tribes, long

before the creation of India and Odisha. The exploitation of natural resources in India runs in the conflict between religious beliefs, and corporatism. A moot question also arises: is India trying to get away from Socialism, which runs deep in the constitutional veins of the legal machinery?

This accumulated injustice has provided a catalyst, for a stark class divide, which has formed a basis, for an armed war, between the State, and its people.

In 2008, a report *'Development Challenges in the Extremist Affected Areas,'* was submitted by an expert group, directed by the Planning Commission of India.

It ascertained the popularity of Maoism, amongst landless peasants, and *adivasis,* and even found some positive implications.

The report rejects the official 'security-centric' approach in dealing with the movement, and instead suggests an 'ameliorative approach with emphasis on a negotiated solution'.

It seems to be a very far cry, from the single biggest internal security rhetoric challenge, posed by the central government.

The Bauxite materialism cause is like ravaging an 85 per cent community and pleasing the rich. To please the corporate fundamentalists, the ruling government, especially the home minister, is urging to make the State a police state.

In a recent outcry, by Arundhati Roy in 2009, in her reportage book, *'Broken Republic,'* the author pondered: 'if it takes 60,000 people to silence tiny valley of Kashmir, how many will it take to contain the mounting rage of hundreds of millions of people?

'If Chidambaram is going to Climate Change Conference this year (2009), can he leave the bauxite in the mountains?'

In the book, *Out of This Earth: East India Adivasis and the Aluminium Cartel (2010),* Samarendra Das and Felix Padel researched, and found out, that the total value of bauxite deposits in Odisha is around \$2.27 trillion at 2004 prices (which would be \$4 trillion till 2009).

The desperation of stakeholders, in the mineral-rich states, is such that there are MoUs signed, at the behest of corporate leaders, at the price of religious beliefs, and environmental degradation.

The CSR debate is underlined for financial profits. Social value and environmental value that should be strategised, in their corporate missions are downplayed, purely for gains.

Having said this, Vedanta's social development debate has not stopped.

Vedanta claimed running initiatives like starting a school, a childcare centre, and tarring of roads but has only been opposed by stiff opposition.
Many academics have now turned to debate, where they critic Maoist struggles, derived from Che-inspired guerrilla war textbooks.

When we talk about *Adivasis*, they have had a history of resistance against the state, which predates Maoism. Now the real test has started for the Indian state.

Is the murder of its people, through Operation Green Hunt, a sane exercise, for the eradication of social ills, from the country? Historically, companies have always won the war, when it comes to displacing people.

The Maoists are waging war on the streets because the impoverished community members are getting displaced, and some of them rarely get jobs. When they get displaced, hopeless, and downtrodden, the movement takes up arms.

Conversely, *Adivasis* and other tribals have the protection of their cultural life, secured through the Indian Constitution.

7 May, 2014

60

WAR AND STATES

WHAT IS CAUSING THESE ENDLESS WARS, in terms of socialist perceptions in our modern world?

Many powerful politicians, especially from the West, have been said to have betrayed their ideals. Often what is articulated by powerful politicians, before they come into power, has not come true.

Socialism has been a moral scale for human upliftment. It has been a great intellectual reminder, practised in our world, which gave the world new, and credible forces of democracy, power to the working class, and several welfare initiatives, that produced several social dimensions, which deserve to get instituted, in a so-called ideal state, for the workers.

However, these ideas have not been practised well, always. Any form of conflict, obstructing a ruling state, bears testimony to this.

There are certain rules as well. Workers see themselves as committed, to some form of radical change, through various political parties, that are given birth, through various ideas.

Nigel Harris believes that armed struggle forms the basis for winning power. Once that power is achieved, people also see new oppressors.

We also see states using military power to suppress people, and so on. This is a profane cycle in Marxism. We have also seen states being made instruments of slavery, and oppression, where several rights are targeted, where poverty, unemployment, bad economic structures, and ignorance loom, and where citizens are discriminated against and marred from their rights. This never implemented the ideas of socialism.

Many modern states have been war economies as well. They want to emancipate their powerful states, through every welfare measure, every social right, every economic reform, and every productive political deal, but have different perceptions on other countries: they plunder and fight for oil, some want to arm rebels there, some want to overthrow governments, some want to kill other politicians, and some simply target civilians, in other countries. In the guise of bringing stability, they collaborate with ruling governments, overthrow, and bring their new puppets into power.

This form of shoddy morality was never right. Several charismatic thinkers of socialism would have never endorsed it, to say the least. They have forgotten the adages, where thinkers, like Marx, believed in the universality of worker reform.

The world is now abuzz with stories of immigrant discrimination, that do not allow new people, to integrate into their new societies, justly, due to a sense of social-cultural orientations. Racism also is a bad form of oppressing certain people. Modern states could use better policies, in helping poorer nations, but they do not.

The megalomania of Obama's administration, or his

predecessor, do narrate a sort of neo-fascist, and neo-imperial agenda, in recent times, by a sort of characterless politicians, who impose bloodshed by being mad with pride, and due to the power, they enjoy from their Senates. The United States, for example, has spent two hundred years in militarism. They forgot that nationalism, in the end, carries no higher value. It is just a form of community cohesion of certain cultural, and other social traits.

These endless wars are fought against the state because an individual, or a certain group, lose their faith, in the ruling state, due to certain paradigms, that constitute, such a functioning state.

Our world is reminiscing the bad ways of the past, like Spanish conquistadors in Latin America, using indigenous labour, and resources for their booties, in the guise of feudalism, for their mother country, under socialism.

Unfortunately, blood has been spilt to bring changes in the world, and it will continue in these modern times as well.

People have lost faith in the systems of their nations, and in globalisation, which is also driven by certain controversial agendas. That is why we see rebel groups fighting against the governments.

Lenin openly theorised war the guns by certain people, who made sure that these ruling people never come back into power. This loss of faith set the standards for a new change, a perception, having convergences, in the thoughts of Mao and Che.

Engels thought that people in minority would bring the new change, who are the rebels. People who demand change.

But war does not define socialism, there were many thinkers, who wanted to bring a bloodless change, but, unfortunately, wars have been a means, a pivotal cause for achieving power. That is how war and states come in contact.

5 January, 2015

61

TRUMPS'S TRUMP CARD

Republican presidential candidate Donald Trump has taken religious bigotry and xenophobia to a new level. He wants to close mosques and monitor the Muslim population. His speeches are uncalled for political actions intended to further disintegrate the minority American Muslim population.

The American perceptions of justice are not universally accepted everywhere. His speeches for Presidential mileage have resulted in a gloating war against Muslims. It also means that American ideas of liberty are merely empty talks. World's second largest religion cannot be practised freely in America. He also wants a database where all Muslims are ought to register their identities. Donald Trump is making shallow assumptions that America is only suffering politically and socially because of Muslims.

His message had come in the wake of a deadly shooting by ISIS-inspired extremists who were involved in a mass shooting in San Bernardino, California. These events do roil the conscience, but as a minority population in America, not all Muslims adhere to the belief system of Islamic State and Al-Qaeda.

One cannot make an entire community responsible for these dauntless murders. Many Muslims are upstanding citizens and highly skilled immigrants contributing to the various sectors of the American economy. Does this mean that post 9/11, far right Americans and the media fascination with it have made Muslims open villains in their new public policy? There is a vilification of Muslim culture going on in America.

Several candidates condemned his proposal to ban Muslims from entering the US, with candidate Jeb Bush referring to Trump's ideas as 'unhinged'. Trump's ideas are further giving a rift between Islam and the west. It is also flaring the undertaking of extremists by reinforcing their narratives.

Marco Rubio, a Republican nomination believes that West is in a 'clash of civilisation' with Islam. This has made minorities in America, especially the Muslims not equal to others. The US can become an exemplar of unity and justice provided it chooses to do so.

America has had a history of slavery, despite attempts for emancipation. There are still racial tensions between blacks and the whites and structural injustices. American history has had a shameful period of discrimination against minorities, a rogue foreign policy, anti-Catholic prejudices, internment of Japanese- Americans and turning away to Jewish refugees who flew the Nazis.

America has a civilian population of 270 million who hold guns. It means it has 50% more firearms per capita. To add more facts, it is not the Muslim population that generally own the guns, but the white men do. Only 32 percent of the American population are white men, but 61 percent of them own guns. Cities like Chester, Pennsylvania, Detroit, Michigan and Camden, New Jersey have highest homicides, which necessarily do not involve Muslims. To make matters worse, gun crime is prevalent in America than any other country.

People need to make a choice to reject fear mongering. Throughout America, attitudes towards Muslims are mixed. Islamophobia is not widespread, but it is prevalent among certain groups and in certain locations. Shortly after the shootings in San Bernadino, California, a Reuters/Ipsos poll found that '51 percent of Americans view Muslims living in the United States the same as any other community, while 14.6 percent are generally fearful'.

Rather than instilling fears, leaders need to construct constructive spaces for discussions. A leader needs to inspire all sections of the society. A modern society is grounded in the insignia of enlightenment, values, and retrospection. Donald Trump has shown no political correctness. On the contrary, his statements are immature. Rather than measuring the equity of the plural character of his State, he is trying to distance the minorities and is making them alien. To be clear, he is trying to make Muslims in America less American than the rest.

December 11, 2015

62

MILITARISM IN KASHMIR

KASHMIR IS LIKE AN OPEN PRISON. The people are captives of caged aspirations.

On roads, the convoys of armies, look like caravans of modern warfare. Their ammunition is a grave scourge.

Militarisation has been harsh to the civil way of life, in Kashmir, because people have seen raging soldiers, lingering around the block after block. Kindness is gone from the land, the truth has been tortured, and people continue to get humiliated.

It is said that there was a time when 35 Rashtriya Rifles used to give a 'cash for corpses incentive scheme,' to its battalion members, through which even innocents have been killed, because no one was asked whom the gunman fired.

Today, India claims to be the world's largest democracy. It takes pride, in its written constitution, its secularity, and the promised reforms to economic prosperity, but acts as a rogue state, when nationalism becomes a preferred doctrine, to subdue the oppressed craving for liberation.

It holds for the poor working class of farmers, the tribals, who with the result of impoverished poverty, have waged a war through guerilla warfare, against the Indian army, in distant lands where economic development, education, and a happy life, seem like a distant dream.

It also holds true for the Kashmiri masses, who have been entangled, in a cyclical form of totalitarianism, through force, after each mass protest.

In the last sixty years, Kashmir has seen the birth of armed insurgencies, and secessionist institutions, inspired by religious and secular nationalism.

It has been seen in numerous martyrdoms of youth, whose blood has been spilt through Palestinian Arab-inspired resistance of stones, the new eastern *intifadah*.

During turbulent times, Kashmir is reduced to deserted streets, due to exaggerated fear. When Kashmir is locked for months, even buying essential commodities becomes an arduous task. A whole generation has lost family members, either killed or disappeared, with no official records.

Unmarked graves run into thousands in Kashmir, which are only researched by international humanitarian organisations, like Amnesty International, and Human Rights Watch, and local research centres, like the Association of Parent of Disappeared Persons, and International People's Tribunal on Human Rights and Justice in Kashmir.

The Indian government pays no heed to all these tragic developments. All these problems are direct offshoots of militarism.

Today, wars have left every country bereft of peace. It has laden every continent, be it Europe, Latin America, Africa, or Asia.

In Kashmir, violence has run unabated towards its people, as well. Militarism has represented a threat to regional integration, and its ethnonational social consciousness.

When we go back to European history, militarism was seen as an instrument of social restructuring, a prerogative to achieve a higher status. In Greece, joining the military reflected bravery. British achieved nobility by joining the military.

The Americans joined the military to achieve respect. It was a means for class inflation. Mostly, countrymen joined the military, due to patriotism, the exaltation of military virtues, and its ideals.

However, militarism, in the world, today, has acquired a different meaning.

The primacy of nationalism creates an advent of conflicts, and that is the reason militarism today is taken in a negative sense. Today, many activists and academia believe that wars are natural consequences of extreme forms of nationalism.

Oscar Wilde once called blind nationalism the trait of the vicious. The lines do hold significance for current neo-fascist states. It is primarily because of the excesses of human rights violations, done, due to militarism, the world over.

In Kashmir, the fatality figures run into hundreds of thousands that even dispute the official records. These realities have transformed Kashmir into a serious conflict zone.

The Indian state has taken Kashmir in larceny, after it promised a referendum, to its people, once Indian authorities signed the provisional accession, with the Maharaja, during the partition era.

Since then, both countries have installed military establishments, divided our lands, separated families, and created an ambience of hostility towards each other. Hence, militarisation has resulted in adverse effects in Kashmir, just like in other conflict zones.

Stockholm International Peace Research Institute (SIPRI) calls India, the largest importer of arms, between the year 2007, and 2011.

The whole weaponry business has resulted in a thirty-seven per cent increase. In the next decade itself, the country plans to invest around a hundred billion dollars, in weapons.

The country is buying arms and ammunition, improving technology, and sharing diplomatic ties with many pivotal defence exporters, like the United States and Germany.

Military strategists are even pressing the governments in power, to modernise its army. These initiatives will further rarify the political developments, needed for the settlement process.

It will even increase the scope of war outbreaks, will further penalise the obedience to UN resolutions, and will neglect peace, due to conflicting bilateralism.

The vale is already the most militarised zone in the world. People live amongst barbed wires, frisking, bunkers, searches, curfews, and interrogations, in a mundane manner.

A former princely state, the valley is now coined as a

disputed legacy, between India and Pakistan, where a resolution seems elusive, even after sixty-five years.

In the troubled times of today, wars against the state, have been reduced to innumerable corpses. George Orwell, the eminent British journalist, rightly believed that totalitarianism is a disease in any state.

In India, the role of the state has grown inequitably stronger, due to nationalistic ideals. Kashmir is India's most volatile occupation. It is because, leaders in the valley, hold a politics of variance.

Some leaders affirm to debate for a resolution, outside the ambit of Indian and Pakistani constitutions, and some glorify violence by sympathising with the armed struggle. India and Pakistan, despite given warnings by UN resolutions, have failed to arrive, at any solution.

Contrarily, both countries have imposed their machinery and insured it with military power. That is why Kashmir remains inured into bloodshed.

16 November, 2012

63

INTROSPECTION ON KASHMIR CONFLICT

KASHMIR HAS BEEN TRANSFORMED INTO A wretched conflict from a beautiful vale, to a wretched conflict, like a despondent poet, blossoming in pain, reciting ballads of war, and violence.

Only failures have made political history here, awakening the memory of death, and suffering every hour, amidst the countless, helpless victims of the conflict.

Kashmir is a land of failed political conjectures, broken dreams, caged liberation, and frenzied mistrust.

Words like 'hope,' 'agreements,' and 'developments' have existed here, but only as rich rhetoric, through various political commentators, and knavish leaders.

Ever since the conflict intensified, Kashmir has become the literary obsession of various observers, historians and activists, whose dissent has been faced, with strong confrontation.

The scope for visionary introspection has been weakening, like a senile old man, struggling to resist.

Kashmir has been perceived as an independent state, a part of India, a part of Pakistan, an autonomous region, a region with permanent borders, divided through a Line of Control, a demilitarised domain, under the control of UN peacekeeping forces, a state emerging through a unitary plebiscite, with or without external mediation.

Still, no firm determination, or unshakable resolution has ever been witnessed, in any debating chamber of Indian, and Pakistani diplomats.

The reasons are obvious. India does not want Pakistan to fiddle in what it deems to be its personal affair, and vice versa.

This remains the main theme of contention, between the two nations, whenever they talk terms and try to ensconce the encumbering emotional baggage, of discontent Kashmiri people, who expect an unhesitant answer, ever since the Indo-Pak partition unleashed misery, and violence subverted peace, of daily life.

As time passes, India is now attempting to completely move away, from calling the Kashmir issue, any dispute, at all. In recent years, governance and elections have been taken, as a final resolution.

Any discourse attempted is taken into consideration, only under the ambit of the Indian constitution. Western countries and Indian allies are viewing the problem, as silent spectators, due to their geo-strategical, and economic interests.

Reasoned debate has also started to get eroded. Many Hindu nationalist intellectuals have been rewriting history, and projecting India, as a Hindu country, rather than a secular country.

This propaganda has concerned Pakistan, about the Muslim brethren, across the Line of Control, which has also given political mileage to extremists, and radical elements, inside Pakistan.

The biggest problem, in Indo- Pak resolutions, is that they take short-term solutions, for the Kashmir dispute, without any representative participation, of the Kashmiri people.

It has altered any good faith in evolving a national consensus, which has such deep-rooted historic, religious, and emotional significations.

A clear public opinion, of the majority, needs to be institutionalised and revolutionised.

The psychological attitude, pertaining among Kashmiris, is that they feel occupied. There is no substitute for a resolution, other than a sincere dialogue, and a process of self-determination.

Kashmiris are frustrated, due to a lack of political freedom, for decades, and are saddled with social and economic grievances.

It has made the need for a resolute resolution more pressing. Unless someone will not recognise the depths of these wounds, it will only help in facilitating brinkmanship, and belligerence.

23 May, 2011

64

SOLUTION IS POSSIBLE

THE FATALITIES IN KASHMIR ARE FAST reaching a six-digit figure. Yet, the levels of fatalities, do not seem to stimulate a genuine peace process, for both hostile neighbours.

The history of Kashmir has not facilitated a resolution, in the past, and given the situation, is unlikely going to do so, in future as well.

Without pleading allegiance to both countries, no political institution is allowed to represent the aspirations of the people, which have been already eroded time, and time again, due to a lack of genuine representation.

The present spatial attributes of resolution are clear: a relationship should continue to be based on centralised power structures, from New Delhi and Islamabad.

The current arrangement, directly or indirectly, predetermines the accession to Pakistan, and India, respectively. Several international independent analysts and agencies have stated that elections have never been held freely, and are largely against the will of the people.

At the same time, there have been no international amendments, in practicality, to bar these 'rig vote' practices.

Unlawful arrests, draconian laws, life-threatening emergency powers of Disturbed Area Act (DAA), Special

Armed Forces Protection Act (AFSPA), in Kashmir, and all versions of torture, continue as natural laws.

How do we expect a resolution possible or Kashmir to develop, when the conditions created, are hostile to safety, by both India and Pakistan?

Humanitarian bodies like Human Rights Watch or Amnesty International are already concerned about these levels of vehement violence and unethical draconian laws that have affected thousands of Kashmiris, emotionally, politically, and economically.

Endorsement of legal powers, by international conventions, which safeguard rights-liberties, and redistribute attributes of sovereignty, is needed through genuine evolution from political actors, of both countries.

Post 1990s, the 'Azaadi sentiment' has acquired a major role, in ensconcing the dispute, for the process of accommodation. But the biggest hindrance faced by the people is that the leaders have succeeded, in evolving a 'trait of flexibility,' in their ideas, for the fear of getting irrelevant. This has unfortunately created an environment of mistrust, and social fragmentation.

The concept of 'Azaadi' should address the Kashmiri standpoint, through a tri-partisan solution, by balancing the political, legal, and social persuasions of the people. 'Internal sovereignty' is more important than concepts of autonomy and self-rule. This is the main reason, why many attempts regarding the implementation of prevailing ideas have failed.

An accomplishable resolution can be implemented by enabling an environment of phased demilitarisation, revocation of all draconian laws, development of new prototype political structures, a ceasefire between armed groups and Indian armed forces, within the region, engagement of domestic armed groups, in a dialogue process, and shared economic integration.

Sadly, the state of India and Pakistan, both, have failed to genuinely address the issue so far, because they have been provided with a 'liberty of multiple interpretations.

The only substitute for dialogue is violence. Every day, when these leaders delay talks, violence continues.

The best method in decreasing the level of violence is through peaceful negotiations. It is a long-term concept for establishing peace. However, there have been no hints of international intervention, and their role has been resisted by mere spectators.

State violence has badly dented the very essence of 'Azaadi,' by hijacking our social domain.

Leaders are slaves to the prevailing sentiment and have crossed all ideological extremes, to facilitate an invalid democratic establishment. This is a harsh reality.

Massive human rights violations have worsened the situation, even further. There are lessons to learn, for India and Pakistan. The world has seen civilised means of resolution. Very recent of which has been *'The Good Friday Agreement*,' which was designed in sound British political machinery. It is in this agreement genuine negotiations replaced guns, to resolve a political conflict, over self-determination. This arrangement ended a violent war, between the British and the Irish, and a resolution model like this could result in the success of Kashmir's resolution.

There have been various attempts, by both countries, to isolate Kashmiris, in pursuit of a resolution, which is unlikely going to succeed. There should be a joint solution that needs to be institutionalised.

Developed leaders, from both sides, unfortunately, have been prisoners of their rhetoric.

There has been no genuine civilised interaction between the two countries.

Wars have been fought, negotiations have been carried out, pacts have been signed, an armed movement is still on, and yet, a decisive outcome is still elusive.

In Kashmir, there is only one concept of genuine leadership. The concept relies heavily on the right of self-determination.

It should be implemented according to the Articles drafted in International Covenant on Civil and Political Rights [ICCPR] and the International Covenant on Economic, Social and Cultural Rights [ICESCR].

India and Pakistan could try to resist practices, which suit their interests and design a valid democratic process, rather than installing leaders directly.

The most unfortunate part is that there is no evidence that India and Pakistan have followed any pattern, or implementing stage worth emulating, in resolving the dispute, because starting a resolution, and then ending up with a blame game, by just signing rhetorical pacts, and empty talks, cannot ultimately yield anything.

3 July, 2010